THE AWAKENING
VALLEY

THE AWAKENING VALLEY

BY JOHN COLLIER, JR.
AND ANÍBAL BUITRÓN

THE UNIVERSITY OF CHICAGO PRESS

THE UNIVERSITY OF CHICAGO PRESS, CHICAGO 37
Cambridge University Press, London, N.W. 1, England
W. J. Gage & Co., Limited, Toronto 2B, Canada

DEDICATION

TO

ROY E. STRYKER *for years of opportunity and encouragement*   J. C.

AND

DONALD COLLIER & JOHN MURRA *for their inspiration and continuing friendship*

A. B.

CONTENTS

THE VALLEY AND THE PEOPLE

OTAVALO

THIS is the valley of Otavalo in Ecuador. Here in the Andean high-lands Indians have lived for many centuries. Throughout the Andes eight out of ten people are Indians. They are the destiny of Ecuador, Peru, and Bolivia—but also a national burden, for here the Indians live in extreme poverty. Ever since the Spanish conquest the Indians have worked in bondage, robbed of their freedom, in a life of hopeless toil. Even today the pattern is little changed. The injustices to the Indians have been perpetuated through ignorance, prejudice, and social decay.

But in the valley of Otavalo there has been an awakening, a miracle of cultural rebirth. The Indians of Otavalo are rising in a wave of vitality that is breaking the bonds of their traditional poverty, making them into a society of prosperous and independent citizens.

· The rise of the Indians of Otavalo is a unique story. Yet the Indians of the Awakening Valley are not different from other Indians. The success they have achieved could be shared throughout the Andes, for their vitality is born of universal energies. Theirs is a story of simple people, a story of day-by-day strength, skill, joy, and faith.

2

THE INDIANS OF THE VALLEY

THE MARKET

DAWN in the Andes. Icy wind sweeps down from the jagged peaks that rim the world. Imbabura towers across the cloudless east. Cotacachi bars the west, her snow crest glowing in the first light. Beneath, night still clings to the valley, wreathing the villages and fields in mist, reaching up the mountains in opulent folds.

For the Indians in the highlands, day comes before darkness has gone. Under the stars they leave their homes at the foot of Imbabura, shoulder their massive burdens, and start their journey downward to market in the valley below.

Saturday morning. The trails leading to Otavalo are crowded with old and young pressing forward at a run, their bare feet moving noiselessly over the dusty paths. Everywhere there are lines of burdened Indians coming from every quarter of the mountain-ringed world. Down over footpaths that join trails, trails that converge into roads, roads that pour into the market town like streams till the streets of Otavalo become an endless river of dark-blue ponchos, bright-red ponchos, brilliantly striped with gold and green and turquoise.

The trails leading from the highlands are worn to deep canyons. The ancient stairways descending into the city are hollowed by centuries of hurrying feet. For the market is very old. The people of the town will tell you that it is old. Their great-grandfathers were born near the market square. But it is older than that by hundreds and hundreds of years. Long before the Spaniards came, there had been a market in the valley. Even before the Incas came, it was there. Since the beginning of now-forgotten time, the Indians have been getting up with the dawn, shouldering their burdens, and descending into the valley of Otavalo to trade.

Before the coming of the Spaniards, traders from distant parts of Ecuador carried their wares to the market. Indians from the far headwaters of the Amazon brought native cotton and *achiote*, the red seeds of a tropical tree which are still used today for coloring food. They brought parrots, monkeys, and strange herbs from the jungle to trade with the highland Indians for salt, blankets, and dogs.

12

Down this ancient cobblestoned street generations of Indians have passed on the way to market.

Today the Indians still trade their blankets with travelers from far away, but now it is for money with which to buy iron plow blades, hoes, and axes. The strangers are for the most part white men and mestizos (of mixed Indian and white blood), who have gotten up with the dawn to trade with the Indians.

During the week the Indians—men, women, and children—work industriously in their own homes preparing articles for the Saturday market. Each community has some specialty to sell. Ponchos of the heaviest wool to guard against the intense Andean cold. Heavy wool shawls for the women of the highland valleys. Woolen cloth of many varieties, woven belts, blankets. Cotton homespuns, worn by all the Indians. Rope made from the fiber of the *cabuya* cactus. Mats and fans fashioned from lake rushes. Baskets and hats made from split cane. Pottery cooking pots and diverse other household utensils. Vegetables, grains, maize, beans, and fat green *haba* beans. Chickens and eggs. Salt, bread, meat, and fat.

The white man also brings his wares to trade. Every temptation is offered to attract the sucres of the thrifty Indians. Bolts of factory-made cloth. Aniline dyes of all hues that are sold by the pinch. Kerosene to light their mountain homes. Cheap jewelry, iron- and tinware. Leather goods, mirrors, needles, spices, and medicinal remedies. Every article has its customary place in one of the four market squares, week after week, year after year.

The first long rays of sunlight find the market already in full swing. In one broad plaza almost all the buyers and sellers are Indian. Men with ponchos to sell occupy one long row at the edge of the square. Each Indian has placed his ponchos on a cotton cloth on the ground and stands behind them against the wall waiting patiently for customers, confident that his handiwork is known and sought after throughout Ecuador. A customer examines the quality, size, and color, asks the price, makes an offer, pretends to go looking for a better bargain, returns and offers a few sucres more. Finally, seller and buyer reach an agreement, and the transaction is completed. Among the crowd there are dealers who buy as many of the ponchos and other woolen goods as they can carry. These dealers come to the Otavalo market early in order to choose quietly and avoid too many competitors. By seven o'clock the best ponchos, shawls, and woolen suitings are gone, and the dealers are already on their way to other markets of the Ecuadorian highlands as far north as Tulcán and as far south as Loja.

In the row next to the ponchos there are woolen materials which copy English tweeds. These are hand-spun and hand-woven to sell to the white world of big

15

The general market
plaza at Otavalo

cities—Quito, Bogotá, and even far-off Caracas. In the same row there are the great shawls which the conservative white and mestizo women of the small towns wear, just as did their early Spanish ancestors. In another row are the rectangles of dark-blue or black flannel that the Indian women buy for their wrap-around skirts and shoulder shawls. Then come the blue-and-white cotton head-cloths called *fachalinas;* the heavy cotton homespun cloth for making petticoats, shirts, and trousers; and the broad and narrow belts worn by all Indian women. Farther along is the raw wool which Indian dealers have brought from the large estates of the next valley. Beyond are the rush mats and fans woven by the Indians from the vicinity of Lake San Pablo. At the back of the market are pottery dishes, cooking pots, water jugs, and large flat plates for toasting corn. These are made by mestizos or by a few Indians from the community of Peguche. On one side of the plaza, in the shade of the tall palm trees, Indian-made whole-wheat bread is on sale, together with a few onions and cabbages and other hot ready-to-eat foods.

Several blocks up the street from the Indian plaza is the big general market. Here in the first row there are vegetables, raised for the most part by Indian gardeners on white property. Beyond are booths offering salt, the rendered fat of beef, sheep, or swine, and meat both raw and cooked. Next is a row of spices, remedies, and charms. These include beaks of eastern jungle birds, the hoofs of animals from the high mountains and low jungles, fruits, and seeds of strange forms and colors, herbs, insects with iridescent wings. Ask a vendor what any one of these things is good for, and invariably he answers, "For heart trouble."

Near by whites and mestizos are selling white bread, corn and beans cooked and raw. Next come bright piles of oranges, bananas, and pineapples brought from the tropical valleys beyond the mountains. Then there are the blacksmiths selling picks, axes, knives, scissors, and iron tips for the wooden plows. All these articles may have been transformed from the chassis of an old truck. Then come the tinkers with pails, kettles, and lamps of various kinds. Next are the jewelers from the near-by town of Cotacachi selling copper rings set with bits of colored glass, cylindrical copper beads, earrings made of old and modern coins, silver and copper pins. Leather workers, also from Cotacachi, are there with pocket-books and belts. Across the way are those who offer embroidered blouses, aniline dyes, and colored thread. Beyond are the vendors of potatoes and sweet potatoes, red carrots and white carrots.

18

In his special spot where all may find him stands the policeman who has charge of the official balance. It is his duty to check the weights given in the market.

Under the arcade which runs along one side of the plaza, vendors display for sale a gay selection of cotton and woolen yard goods from Ecuadorian factories or imported from Colombia or the United States. Ready-made clothes, mirrors, gilded beads and corals, marbles, belts, and needles are here too.

Around the corner under a small lean-to, Indian women are cooking soup in big kettles over wood fires. Into the soup they put the heart, lungs, liver, and intestines of the cattle and sheep, parts which the whites refuse to eat. The Indians relish this soup and devour great bowls of it here at the "kitchen" or carry it home in jars.

In this general market three-fourths of the people are Indians, a proportion which holds true for all the region. It is to this plaza also that the housewives of Otavalo come to buy their weekly supplies. Among the colorful crowd of Indians in red and blue ponchos these women can be seen, carefully wrapped in their black shawls or wearing modern overcoats. Each is followed by a servant carrying the big market basket. Here and there the women stop to bargain, often calling a policeman to oblige a vendor, usually Indian, to lower her price. As soon as their shopping is finished, they hurry away from the crowded plaza.

Standing on a table above the crowd is a traveling salesman, a ventriloquist whose doll laughs and talks to his audience, selling them a marvelous medicine guaranteed to close any wound, priced at one sucre the bottle. Farther on is a fortune-teller with a cage full of sparrows. For ten cents he will have a bird pick up one of the little bits of folded paper with your fortune written on it. Friars in brown and white habits carry the small statue of a saint up and down the plaza to be kissed by the devout, who drop a coin through the hole in its base. An Evangelist minister, a "gringo," illustrates a passage from the Bible with colored pictures and distributes pamphlets to his listeners.

Beside the Indian market and the general market there are two animal markets, one where small animals such as pigs and sheep are sold, the other for horses, cattle, mules, and burros.

In the early-morning sunlight each market is a swirl of color, a formless pattern that fills the square like the flooding tide. Dark-red ponchos, wine-purple, deep-blue, mixing with magenta shawls, cherry-red shoulder cloths, electric-

19

blue and emerald-green shoulder cloths, white hats and brick-red hats, white shirts and pants of homespun cotton, blouses embroidered with bright and harmoniously blended colors, the flashing red of coral and gilded beads. . . .

But soon after eight o'clock most of the purchases have been made and bargains closed, and the sea of hats begins ebbing away, spreading through the many streets of the town. Now the straight-spaced lines of vendors and stalls can be distinguished. The white canvas booth tops catch the growing glare of the sun. Lingering crowds gather in knots, gossiping and arguing. The vendors count their money. A hungry dog slinks along the ground looking for food. The market is over.

But still the Indians linger in Otavalo. Saturday is the day to see the world, to dance and sing in the taverns, to drink the fiery sugar-cane rum. It is the day to bring a chicken or a basket of eggs to a *compadre*, the white godfather of one's children. Hours can be passed thus, sitting on a cool porch, listening to the white man advise and condemn and explain the countless problems that beset an Indian in a white man's world. While the men discuss and smoke, the Indian women watch with devoted admiration as the *señora* of the house deftly embroiders a skirt or blouse for them on her magical sewing machine. Other Indians visit their lawyers about a lawsuit that has been going on for months concerning a lost title, a drunken fight, the theft of an ax. Others, kneeling silently in the darkened church, place a candle at the feet of a favorite saint, asking his help.

Down in the deserted market square, flies buzz contentedly over the refuse of decayed fruit and discarded bones. A policeman rounds up a few straggling Indians, takes their ponchos or hats as "tokens," and orders them to sweep the plaza to redeem their belongings.

Indians in the valley raise onions and cabbages which they sell to the farmers who live up on the mountain.

From all over the valley Indians come to market. They have walked miles over the dusty trails and are in no hurry to turn homeward. They stand and watch the crowd and linger over each purchase.

The master of the scales, impartial mediator of a thousand disputes. Standard weight is insured by this municipal policeman, who checks suspicious weights on a government scale.

Weavers come to the market to buy their wool and the brilliant-hued aniline dyes, which the Indian vendors sell pinch by pinch.

Most of the Indians' clothing is hand woven. Six *varas* of Indian homespun will make a shirt and a pair of trousers.

Every week kerosene must be bought for the tiny oil lamps that light the Indian homes.

Rope in the Andes is made from *cabuya* fiber. The spearlike leaves of this cactus grow along every road and are easily converted into powerful rope and twine.

Clay pots and plates are made in the community of Peguche and sold in the market to all the other Indians of the district.

Salt is rare in the Andes. It is traded from great distances and is so valuable that it often serves as a medium of exchange.

The market is over. Goods have been all sold and bartered, and the Indians pause to talk with friends or to listen to the tales of strangers from far away.

THE JOURNEY HOME

THE sun is high in the heavens. Giant peaks that were sharp against the sky at dawn are now buried in cloud. Deep-blue shadows sweep over the valley, carrying with them the chill of the Andes. Roads which run out from Otavalo like spokes of a wheel are again full of Indians. Top-heavy swaying busses pass in a choking cloud of dust carrying traders away to distant towns. Slowly, swaying under heavy burdens, or driving a reluctant pig, cow, or bull, the Indians begin the long dusty climb over the hills to their homes. As if retracing history, each step carries them nearer the mountain and their ancient pattern of life. Their bare feet leave imprints in the whitish dust of the trail.

The story of the valley is forgotten or buried beyond memory. Indian life in the mountains is very old. Civilization has overtaken civilization like strata layers of an ancient plain. There are legends, ancient customs, place names, and fragments of pottery from which histories have been written—histories of migrations, conquests, and invasions.

A thousand years ago, so legends tell, the Caras, ancestors of the present Otavalos, came as invaders to the valley. By language they were linked with the Chibcha-speaking peoples of Colombia and Central America. It is said that they came from over the sea. They lived and founded cities by the Pacific on the northern coast of Ecuador, on the edge of the steaming jungle. Probably in search of better climate, the Caras migrated up the Guayllabamba River till they reached the Andean plateaus, where they conquered and overran the ancient people called Quitos and spread rapidly northward over the highlands of northern Ecuador. Here the wanderings of the Caras ended. They settled forever beneath the snow-clad peaks of the Andes.

Even in those distant times the Caras were great agriculturists. With their primitive tools of bone, stone, and wood, they cultivated great areas of communal land. It is believed that they raised maize, beans, *quinoa*—a cereal native to the

29

Andes—chocho beans, and tiny bitter cherries. They domesticated guinea pigs and hunted deer, rabbits, and birds. Skilled at weaving, they wove mantles of cotton which they wrapped around their bodies, fastening them at the shoulder with copper or silver pins, girdling them at the waist with bright-colored belts.

Their houses were almost the same as many houses of today, square dwellings made of wattle and daubed with mud, with a high pointed roof of thatched straw. Their way of life was so stable, their agriculture so sound, that, even after they were conquered by the Incas and exploited by the white man, it survived. The Indians still carry out their ancient pattern of planting and harvesting, deeply in harmony with the earth, the cold Andean rains and stormy skies, and the desolate peaks that are the boundary of their world.

In 1455 the Incas, whose powerful empire ruled all Peru and Bolivia, began expanding northward. Nation after nation fell before their armies. First the Paltas, then the Cañaris, the Puruhas, the Panzaleos, and, finally, after sixteen years of bloody struggle, the Caras of Otavalo. The last Cara leader died in battle near the site of Otavalo, and his daughter was taken in marriage by the Inca conqueror, Huayna Capac. Atahualpa, the last ruling emperor of the Incas, was said to be a son of this mating.

The Inca rulers, though in power little more than a half-century in the Otavalo region, reorganized nearly all aspects of the Caras' aboriginal life after a pattern of their own. They introduced their religion, their temples and their monasteries, their priests and virgins of the sun, their many fiestas and liturgies. Inca sun worship was the official religion, but at the same time each conquered group was allowed to worship its own gods, so that the Inca influence was more material than spiritual. The conquered people were organized into self-sufficient groups who worked their own land but also the holdings of the church and state, for in practice all land belonged to the emperor. The people also served in the army and maintained the magnificent system of roads that the Incas developed throughout their realm. In turn, the emperor supplied everyone with food and clothing in case of famine or disaster and in general established a system of benevolence over all the empire.

The Incas further influenced the aboriginal life by the introduction of new foods. They taught the people advanced methods of irrigation and introduced the use of fertilizer, a practice which greatly increased the yield of their fields. The Inca tongue of Quichua was taught as the state language, and the native language of the Caras has since disappeared altogether. Only a few place names are left as reminders of the earlier language.

But the wonderful organization and great expanse of empire of the Incas were doomed to extinction. In the year 1532 Pizarro conquered Peru, and a few years later Captain Sebastián Belalcázar subjugated Ecuador, ending for all time the Indian rule of the Andes.

The Spanish conquistadores came in search of gold. They uncovered little of it in the northern provinces of the Inca Empire, but they stayed to found cities and to possess the land in the name of the crown and the soul of the Indian in the name of the church. Indian resistance was drowned in bloody torture. The highly organized agrarian culture of the Incas was scattered. Indians fled to the cloud-swept high mountain *páramos* and down to the steaming jungles, abandoning their fertile valley lands and even their families to the Spaniards. For three hundred years the Spanish colonial empire exploited the land and enslaved the people. Great tracts of land, haciendas, were held in feudal ownership. The Indians were vassals to the Spaniards, who held over them the power of life or death, decreed their every act, and forced them to work in slavery.

Independence from Spain and the beginning of the Republic of Ecuador meant very little to the Indians, for the hacienda economy continued. What laws have been written for the Indian's protection have not been effective, so that in many places a father's or grandfather's debt still holds the Indian chained to the estate. Today most of the Indians of Ecuador are *huasipungeros*, landless serfs who work and live on an estate in exchange for a miserable daily wage and the use of a plot of land to cultivate for themselves. Others are "peons," free but landless, working out in villages or haciendas for whatever the white people of the region will pay. But there are also Indians who never lost all their lands, communities high on the mountains, who have held to their land with an unrelenting passion.

Otavalo is one of these few communities. For centuries the Indians here have tilled the rocky slopes of Mount Imbabura, ever watching the fertile valleys below them. They see the rich irrigated fields of the haciendas. They eye the great hillside acreages that the hacienda owners have never cultivated. They wait and watch and save with a dogged determination, till eventually their long-hoarded sucres reward them with the land. More than in any other region of Ecuador, the Indians of Otavalo have bought land, shrinking year after year the holdings of

31

the haciendas. For land is a gnawing hunger they carry forever in their hearts. To work to save. To work for land.

Behind Otavalo the long low hill of Reyloma rises, a barrier between the white world and the Indian communities that lie on the slopes of Imbabura and around Lake San Pablo. Highway and railroad circle the long way around in a gentle grade, but the footpaths of the Indians go straight up. Homeward-bound from market, the Indians see the town of Otavalo sharp below them, neat little town of straight streets, whitewashed adobe houses with red tile roofs, steepled churches, and board plazas. This is the pattern the conquering Spaniards brought to the valley four centuries ago, a foreign order that deprived them of their birthright and their valley. Even the little narrow-gauge railroad winding over the hills to Quito binds the Indians' world in its steel bands.

The trail winds over the brow of the hill. Brown *páramo* grassland stretches away on either hand, westward toward Otavalo and the valley haciendas, east-ward toward the mountains and the cold blue waters of Lake San Pablo that like a knife blade shears across the foot of towering Imbabura. The Indians pause, wind fluttering their ponchos like wings. Some put down their burdens. Others, just standing, breathe deeply of the great expanse of cloud and moun-tain. Their lands lie across the lake, a maze of tiny fields and tiny houses that stretch up the flanks of Imbabura in an ever steepening curve.

Each man sees his own home and fields. There is his corn patch, a golden dot in the immense tapestry of crooked walls. And just to the left, how easy it is to see the rich dark earth of the field he plowed just yesterday! So clearly his eyes follow the winding trail that passes his friend's house. Here it is lost in the dark

feather of eucalyptus trees. There it runs again, down through the marshes to the lake. The alien world is forgotten. Before him stretches the bountiful mother earth under the brooding peak of *Taita* Imbabura, father of all mysteries. Before him is his past and his future, destiny that is woven in a timeless pattern of earth and seed and harvest.

Before him is not one community but a series of communities, or *parcialidades*, divided with exactness one from the other by a river, a canyon, a gravel slide. Each community represents a closely integrated pattern of privately owned lands, each holding marked off from its neighbor by hedges of massive cactus and rock and earthen walls. The houses are not gathered together in a village but are scattered over the cultivated fields, each house guarding the holdings of its owner. The fields are usually very small, but every foot is extensively farmed. Every foot must yield its harvest to the devoted labor of the Indian farmer.

A hum of conversation spreads through the group. Laughing, they shoulder their packs and in a long line descend the winding trail that leads to the lake. On either hand fields of wheat ripple in the wind. Everywhere there are neatly hedged fields, fields of beans, fields of corn. And here a hut of wattle and mud, there a modern house of rammed earth with a red tile roof.

The trail dips suddenly, dropping at once to the valley of the lake. Here the hill trail joins the well-beaten road that skirts the shores of Lake San Pablo. The road is crowded with Indians who have chosen the long way around the hill. Many are carrying heavy bundles, but others are walking free, reeling with drink they have consumed at the wayside taverns. Some are sad, talking mournfully to themselves of the thousand wrongs that beset life. But others are singing and shouting, calling out to the mountain, calling out to the sheening lake and the cool green bulrushes waving along the shore, calling out to the grazing cows that stand belly-deep in the crystal-clear water munching marsh grass, calling out to the young girls who are washing by the shore. For they are nearing home. They are happy.

In the center of a newly plowed field stands a house, the beginning and end of all this journey. The weary eyes of the Indian greet it. Each familiar detail is greeted with a loving glance. Its solid earth walls, the particular tilt of its high thatched roof that is like no other. This is not only home; it is the center of all things, all the world, all that life has to give the Indian farmer. Knowingly and quietly he steps across the threshold.

33

The town of Otavalo is the world of the white man. The Indians enter it with distrust and leave it gladly for the peace and oldness of the mountains.

Beyond the last house of the white townspeople, the Indian fields begin, hedged with massive *maguey* cactus.

Much of the valley belongs to wealthy landholders, who often let the lands lie fallow, but the hills belong to the Indians, and every foot is farmed with loving care.

Highways in the Andes twist and turn and waste a lot of time. The Indians prefer their own trails, which follow the birds directly over the hills to home.

Indian fields on
the slopes of
Mount Imbabura

Beyond the bridge begin the fields of the community of La Compañía, which lies at the foot of Mount Imbabura. The Indians are nearly home. They hurry over the bridge eagerly.

Home at last. The Indian returns to the center of his life—his land from which springs all prosperity, and his home which is the end of all labor.

THE INDIAN'S DAY

AGRICULTURE

THE Indians' day is from dawn to twilight. Often they start their daily work in the darkness. Before breakfast they climb the rocky trails to their mountain fields to plow and cultivate while the dew is still on the ground, or to harvest while the morning sun is bright and warm, for by noon storm clouds may gather, cold winds begin to blow, and the misty Andean rain shroud the *páramo* uplands. Five o'clock in the morning, and the farmer is on his way, driving his oxen before him and carrying his wooden plow on his shoulder. He is followed by his wife carrying a hoe and his small son or daughter shouldering a bundle of toasted corn for an early meal in the fields.

The Otavalo Indian, like all the Indians of the inter-Andean plateau, is above all a farmer. His forefathers have worked the land from earliest times. Long before the Incas came they cultivated maize, several types of beans, potatoes, and bitter little cherries. The Incas brought new varieties of root vegetables, *yucas*, *ocas*, sweet potatoes, and peanuts. Later the Spaniards came with a great variety of plants, especially cereals, vegetables, and fruits.

Variety of crops in the Andes is determined not by seasons but by altitudes. In the valley lands and the moist lake shore almost all the crops of the temperate zone flourish—corn, beans, squash, and garden vegetables of many varieties are grown. As the fields spread up the mountain, the ground is drier and the nights cooler. Here corn, beans, and peas are the main crops; but, as the fields ascend, wheat and barley take the place of corn. And still higher, where these European grains will not grow, the native Andean grain, *quínoa*, still flourishes. Many kinds of root vegetables are grown, the varieties changing with the elevation. Finally altitudes of ten and eleven thousand feet stop even the Indian farmer. In these highest fields the only plant that will mature is a tiny potato, no bigger than a peanut.

In pre-Inca times it is likely that the only agricultural tool of the Ecuadorian highlands was the crude digging stick—a pole sharpened at one end and hardened in the fire. With this implement holes could be drilled for seeding and soil loosened around plants without plowing up a whole field. The conquering Incas brought little change to this technique, for they too used a digging stick, but theirs was improved by the addition of a crossbar which allowed the farmer to force the stick into the ground with the weight of his body. The chief innovations of the Incas were neither in tools nor in plants but in agricultural methods. They introduced fertilizer, irrigation canals, and the terracing of hillside fields. The most important contributions of the Spaniards to native techniques were iron tools—the plow, the hoe, the shovel—and the use of traction animals, oxen and horses. Today the Indians use wooden plows with iron tips wrought by the town blacksmiths. They plow with a yoke of oxen, their own or rented.

Planting time is November. This is a month of rains, and, as soon as the moisture has softened the hard lime soil, plowing begins. The farmer plows his field and then plows it again at right angles to the first plowing. Next he harrows the ground with a triangular drag of poles weighted down with stones. Then he leaves the field for two weeks or a month "to rot," and finally he plows it again to form even furrows for planting. Whenever possible the Indians plant at the time of the final plowing. While the farmer urges on the oxen, his wife and children, possibly with the help of a neighbor, walk behind the plow, dropping seeds into the furrows. But if the planting is delayed until the next day, the farmer uses a digging stick or a narrow wooden shovel. He advances along the furrows, making holes at even intervals and placing in each four to six kernels of corn. The wife follows along behind, dropping three or four beans in with the corn, pushing the earth over each hole with her foot. Behind her come the children, who make a second pattern of holes in which they drop three or four fat *haba* beans and cover them over with dirt. Around the border of the field, and sometimes in widely spaced rows between the corn, *quínoa* is planted. Finally, a few squash seeds are broadcast over the planted furrows, and the field is left to the rains.

Soon the field is covered with tender green sprouts, and the family comes again to the plot for the first cultivation, the weeding. With shovels and hoes they level off the furrows, loosening the earth around the weeds, cutting their shallow roots. "Bad weeds" that would take root and grow again are thrown away, but the "good weeds" that will dry quickly are left on the surface to form fertilizer. One month later comes a second cultivation, in which the furrows are formed

50

again with the plow. After another month the plants are hilled with shovel and hoe. This is the last of the three cultivations, each a month apart. Corn planted high on the mountain needs only one cultivation, the weeding one month after planting.

The corn flower and the upper section of the stalk are cut about the middle of March, to prevent the strong winds of April from blowing down the plants. The flower is fodder for the cattle and is often sold in the market. In April the first ears of green corn, *choclos*, are ready. From then until the plants are dry, a jar of green corn is never lacking at the Indian fireplace. By July or August the several varieties of beans have been harvested, some of them while still green, together with the green corn, and the others when dry a little before the maize harvest. The green beans and shelled green corn are boiled together in a succotash called *chiflimote*. This is often sold in town ready to eat. The Indian women also market green *haba* beans, raw or cooked, and green or ripe squash.

During the corn harvest in August, as in all agricultural tasks, the whole family works together. If the field is very large, a few relatives or friends may be invited to help harvest in return for a number of baskets of maize besides their food during the days they work. The harvesters go forth equipped with a mantle whose four corners are tied together and passed over the left shoulder. The sack thus formed hangs below the right arm. Each worker advances in his furrow, bending the stalks, plucking the ears from their husks, and depositing them in the improvised sack. When the sack is full, the Indian returns to the house and piles the corn inside or on the porch. The husks of a few ears are left to be pulled back and tied together in pairs and hung on a pole or cord strung below the roof of the porch or the inside room. The best ears of corn, those with slender cob and fat kernels, are chosen for seed and kept separately. The harvest finished, the Indians form a cross with dry cornstalks and stick it upright in the pile of corn. Poor women may pass through the fields, gleaning occasional ears that have been overlooked on the stalk or have fallen to the ground.

After some days the dry cornstalks are cut with sickles and left scattered on the field drying in small bunches, later to be gathered and formed in a mound called the *parva*. On the day chosen for making the *parva* all members of the family and perhaps a few relatives and friends gather the sheaves of stalks into one place. The head of the house arranges them in a circle, layer upon layer. Sheaf after sheaf is passed to him; soon the mound is so high that the bundles must be tossed

51

up to him as he stands on top gathering and arranging them. Later a ladder is used to carry up the bundles. When the mound is finally finished, it may reach a height of six to nine feet. In this way the cornstalks are stored throughout the year. The livestock, especially oxen and cows, are fed with the dry stalks from August until March. Then the corn is in flower, and there is abundance of grass and corn leaves.

Wheat, barley, chocho beans, *quínoa* grain, lentils, and sometimes peas and *haba* beans are harvested by cutting the stalks or by pulling out the whole plants. These are carried home to finish drying. Later they are scattered in the dooryard and threshed with long poles to open the pods and free the grains. The straw from wheat or barley is formed into mounds like those of cornstalks.

Dry seasons and wet seasons are not the only guides for the Indian farmer. Phases of the moon and days of the week are important. Thursdays and Fridays are the days chosen for planting, for on these days "the birds from heaven" do no harm. It is also considered wise to plant or harvest at least three days after the new moon, for otherwise the seeds or the harvest will rot. Faithful to ancient traditions and customs, the Indian farmer goes about his fields with the authority of generations of devotion and labor. With his pattern of intensive subsistence agriculture, he works peacefully within the balance of nature, his crops as much a part of the land as the *páramo* grass on the mountains or the bulrushes around the lake.

The Indians plow three times to prepare their fields for planting. They use the iron-tipped plow and the oxen the Spanish conquerors brought them four centuries ago.

The Indian's harrow is as simple as his plow—a triangle of lashed poles weighted down with rocks.

Up the mountain to the meadows. An old woman continues her spinning as she leads her flock over the rocky trails.

After plowing, the farmer breaks the clods with a crude hoe.

High on the mountain the Indians plant root plants like potatoes and *ocas*, or cold-country grains like barley and *quínoa*.

In the early morning light Indians hurry homeward. Plowing is done for the day, and at home a multitude of other tasks await them.

Harvested beans, like all crops, are carried home from the mountain on the Indian's back.

Indian fields stretch from the lake shores up the mountain wall as high as altitude permits.

Golden fields of wheat and barley wave in the chill Andean wind.

The Indian fields are small but richly planted. With a hand sickle the farmer harvests his precious crop of barley.

Corn is the staff of life. Each ear is carefully harvested and stored away in the home. The stalks are gathered in mounds for fodder.

HOME TASKS

LIFE moves on continuously around the Indian home. The little house is the hub of everyone's activities; from it all travel in their labors, and to it the produce of all their energy returns. Here they store their grain and beans and the wool for weaving. The thick walls hold their life secure and guard their hard-won prosperity.

The houses of an Indian community are not gathered around a plaza as in Spanish villages. They are scattered over the cultivated fields, each house overlooking its small plot of land. In the communities close to town most of the houses are made of rammed earth and are roofed with Spanish tile purchased in town. In the more isolated communities most of the houses are made of mud and wattle with high thatched roofs of *páramo* grass. The tile-roofed houses are generally larger than the thatched huts, but the plan is the same. Both consist of a single windowless inner room with a small door that leads to a broad open porch. There are no ceilings or floors. In front of the porch is a square dooryard of pounded mud, and near it is a kitchen garden where the Indians grow medicinal herbs, cabbages, a few onions, and—because they are indispensable in the practice of witchcraft—a few carnations.

The open porch of the Indian home is the workshop where most of the daily work is done. Here the light is good for working, the roof gives shade from the glaring sunlight, and the wall of the house wards off the sharp or dusty winds. On the porch of almost every house stands a Spanish loom, an Indian backstrap loom, or both. The millstone is also on the porch, where corn is ground into flour for the daily porridge, or where barley or *chuchuca*—green corn parboiled and dried—is prepared for soup.

The Indians are never idle. They work at a steady unhurried pace, changing occupation from time to time when they tire. While the mother prepares the noon meal, the father may hook up the oxen and plow in the fields near by or hoe the small corn plants. In the heat of the noonday sun he may sit on the

62

porch to weave on a poncho, or a belt, or a length of light wool flannel for a woman's skirt. Perhaps he will twist a little rope of fiber he has dried from the *cabuya* cactus that grows by the wayside. The younger children, boys and girls, take the sheep and swine out to pasture on the hills or along the ravines. The older children work with their parents. The boys learn to farm and to weave. The girls are taught to sew and embroider, to spin wool or cotton with the reed spindle or the spinning wheel, to wash, and to cook.

Spinning and weaving go on all day long in a busy Indian home, for not only are textiles the main source of barter and cash but nearly all the clothing is conventionally homespun and woven. Not every family weaves all the types of Indian cloth, but most families weave some of the many varieties that make up the Indian costume.

Throughout the region of Otavalo the Indians wear essentially the same costume. However, there are many little details of dress that make it possible to distinguish Indians of one community from those of another. For example, in communities far from the towns the Indian women sew all the family clothes, while in communities close to the towns they have many of their clothes made by professional seamstresses on sewing machines.

The Indian man wears shirt and trousers of a heavy white cotton woven on the Spanish loom, or of a similar muslin made in Ecuadorian factories. Indians who live in close contact with town generally have the cuffs and collars of their shirts made of finer white cloth bought in the stores. The seamstresses in town embroider the collar, cuffs, and front of the shirt on the sewing macine, making geometrical designs with gay-colored thread. When the Indians themselves sew the shirts, they embroider the collars and cuffs with little stylized figures—a horse, a dog, a little man, or a sunburst, nearly always in red wool. The short pants reach a little below the knee and are not decorated.

Over this cotton ensemble the Indian man wears one and sometimes two heavy woolen ponchos of brilliant hue. If he is rich, one of these will have two faces, one color on one side, another color when reversed. These ponchos are woven on the pre-Columbian backstrap loom. This gets its name from the broad leather strap by which the weaver buckles himself to the rod that holds the warp. As he leans back on this strap, the weaver provides the necessary tension on the warp. Belts are also woven by the same principle, though the belt warp may be only an inch and a half across.

64

Both men and women wear felt hats, and they are a prized part of the wardrobe. The man's hat may be the typical Indian one of stiff and heavy felt with round or slightly conical crown and broad shallow-curved brim, colored white with cornstarch or red with brick dust. Or his hat may be a European soft felt fedora. Hat styles vary slightly from one community to another. In the communities closest to the towns the fedora is beginning to predominate, especially among the younger men. The women always wear the native stiff felt hat, never the soft European fedora. Now and then the Indian men wear sandals with soles of *cabuya* rope and cloth tops, or simply soles made of hide or old automobile tire bound on the feet with thongs. Women almost never wear sandals of any kind.

The woman wears a long shirt of white homespun or factory-made muslin that reaches nearly to her heels. She herself embroiders this garment around the neck and the short sleeves or hires it done by some Indian or mestizo woman who makes a business of embroidering blouses. In place of the embroidered blouse and petticoat, Indian women in isolated communities often wear a cream-colored or beige rectangle wrapped around the body like a tunic and fastened at the shoulders with silver or copper pins. This tunic answers the description of pre-Spanish dress given by the early chroniclers.

The rest of the Indian woman's dress is made up of rectangles of cotton or woolen material, which may be hemmed on the edges but are not otherwise sewed. This lack of cutting and tailoring points to the antiquity of the styles. Above her combination blouse and petticoat the woman wraps a rectangular piece of navy blue or black flannel to form a skirt, *anaco*, with one side left open for freedom of movement. This flannel may be woven by the Indians themselves or made of finer imported material. The imported material is sometimes embroidered at the lower edge with colored thread in geometrical designs. A rich Indian woman may wear a white flannel skirt underneath the blue or black one. The *fachalina*, a rectangular piece of Indian cotton woven in white or blue-and-white stripes, serves various functions. The woman ties one *fachalina* around her shoulders over her blouse. A second becomes the headcloth which she folds, ties, or twists about her head according to the style of her community. Around her shoulders she also wears a rectangular piece of light wool flannel called a *rebozo*, which, like the flannel of her skirt, may have the lower edge embroidered with colored thread in geometrical designs. Rich women or those near the towns often use imported cloth of bright colors for their *rebozos*—bright blue, red, and various shades of green are the most popular. Those farther away use only the native flannel in dark blue or black. When walking, the woman wears only the cotton *fachalina* over her shoulders, carrying the woolen *rebozo* on top of her hat or over one arm.

The Indian woman's skirt is bound at the waist with two belts. First comes the broad *mamachumbi*, the "mother belt," red with green edges, made of rope and wool and strong like a girdle. Around and around over this the woman winds a long narrow belt of many colors and intricate design, the "baby belt," *guaguachumbi*, or simply *chumbi*. When the woman wears a hat, she places it on top of her *fachalina* headcloth.

No costume is complete without jewelry. Indian women delight in many chains of beads, some gilded and shining, some of coral, some of manufactured red beads. The breast of a rich woman may be piled high with necklaces. From their ears the women hang little chains of natural or imitation corals. Around and around each wrist they wrap a long string of corals or red beads to serve as a bracelet and as a place to tuck coins. Both men and women wear many rings, as many as three or four on each finger of both hands. These rings are generally made of copper, although a few may be of silver. They are set with bits of colored glass.

There is no idleness in the Indian family. Men are in the fields. Women are washing at the lake. Meanwhile industry in the home goes on uninterrupted—spinning and weaving and household tasks that continue from dawn to dusk.

Only the Indians who maintain close contact with the white-mestizo town have their clothes made by the village seamstresses.

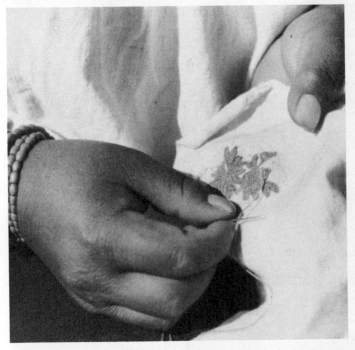

All the others sew for themselves and embroider their blouses skilfully and in good taste.

Indian women are proud of their fine clothes, and, when guests are in the house, they like to wear their best even to perform the simple household tasks.

The first textiles of the Indians were woven of cotton. Today they still spin cotton by the simple hand method they used centuries ago.

Belt-weaving is the simplest and probably the oldest of the surviving textile crafts. Colored belts with geometric designs or stylized figures are an important article of dress for the Indian women.

Every man must have a poncho in the cold mountains of Ecuador. Seated close to the warping bench, the weaver begins to transform the yarn into a beautiful robe.

The backstrap loom with its endless warp is as complicated to operate as it is simple in design. There is just one way to weave a poncho, and it is the way Indians wove ponchos long before the coming of the white men.

Not far from the Indians' homes at the foot of Imbabura lie the glistening waters of Lake San Pablo. Myriad trails lead down to its shores. All day long people come and go, for they love the lake. On any pretext they will drop their work and hurry down to the fringe of cool green bulrushes. Possibly to look after a straying cow, feeding belly-deep in the water cress and lavender-flowering hyacinths.

In the icy lake waters the Indians wash their wool before spinning.

They come to the lake to wash their clothes, to bathe, and to wash out their glistening long hair.

They also come to fill their large clay jars with fresh clear water for the home.

Carrying home a *caballete*, a raft of rushes which the Indians straddle like a horse.

On their rafts the Indians ride out over the lake, paddling through the marshes to look for birds' eggs or herbs or to cut grass and rushes. From the rushes they make mats and fans which whites and Indians from all the canton buy in the weekly market.

FOOD AND REST

BREAKFAST, lunch, and dinner are not absolute divisions in an Indian's day. The early morning meal may be eaten on the mountain while the family rests by the plow—a handful of parched corn as the sun rises out of the mountain. Lunch and dinner are eaten when fatigue and hunger overtake the workers. Sometimes the meals are cooked on the open porch but more commonly in the interior of the house. Always it is simple fare, prepared patiently over a fire of twigs, cornstalks, or cornhusks.

Only the sunlight is warm in the high altitudes of Ecuador, so the inner room of the Indian home is dark and damp with the Andean cold. Near one wall or in the center of the room is the "kitchen," where three stones form a hearth for the cooking fire. Behind it the walls are blackened from the fire. Overhead the rafters are sooty where the smoke finds its way out through a thousand chinks in the tile or thatch. Fuel is scarce in the Andes, and the Indian cooking is simple. Between meals the fire is banked to preserve a few coals for the next fire. Matches are dear, and, if the fire goes out, the housewife will hurry to her nearest neighbor for live coals.

Lined up against the walls, there are jugs of various sizes, wide-mouthed jars for storing water as well as *chicha*, the native drink brewed from fermented corn. Designed to be carried on the back, the jars have conical bases; to stand upright in the house, the jars must be buried in the ground almost to their middles. About the room small pegs are stuck in the wall for hanging garments, skeins of thread or bunches of raw wool, wheels for spinning yarn, and diverse other objects. Around the fire there are clay pots and bowls for cooking, clay plates for toasting corn, and wooden spoons and ladles. These are the indispensable cooking utensils found in every Indian home. Where the Indian kitchen is influenced by white culture, the basic equipment is supplemented by European utensils. Next to the clay pots stand iron caldrons; beside the pottery dishes are one or two of enamelware or china; next to the wooden spoons are some of metal.

Tostado, parched corn, is the staff of life. The women must toast it every day, for it can never be missing from the Indian table.

At one end of the room a ladder leads to a platform made of cane or bamboo, which rests on the walls of the house below the roof. Here corn and other food is stored, safe and dry. In one corner of the room there is a smaller lower platform of cane, on which a mat, a hide, and several old ponchos are piled. This is the Indian bed. In some communities the Indians sleep in the center of the room next to the fire, which smolders all the night. In others they sleep on the porch on a rush mat or hide. Opposite the door a niche is hollowed out of the wall where the Indians keep any religious articles they may have.

Guinea pigs run back and forth in the inner room. One or two dogs doze on the porch or in the dooryard. Chickens forage about for food, roosting at night on the branches of a *lechero* tree or on a pole tied under the eaves of the house for that purpose. In the corners of the porch, high on the wall, hang baskets lined with a little straw where the hens lay their eggs.

Maize is the basic diet of all the Indians. Those in communities far from town exist almost entirely on the products of their own land, buying only a little salt or fat or a few onions in the market. Those who live in communities near the towns almost always supplement their home-grown foods with extras or varieties from the stores and market places.

Every day the Indian housewife climbs to the storage platform to fill a basket with ears of dried corn. She shells the kernels, starts the fire, and sets the clay toasting plate on the three hearthstones. She feeds the fire with dry cornstalks, with cobs, or with dry branches that she herself has gathered with the help of husband or child in the ravines or high on the mountain. On the broad flat toasting plate she sprinkles a handful of corn and stirs it with a wooden spoon or a corncob. Her movements are precise and rhythmic. The corn on the plate moves around and around, toasting uniformly. From time to time she blows up the fire with a hollow reed until at last the corn is parched a golden brown. She pours this toasted corn, *tostado*, into the basket to cool and carefully replaces the plate against the wall.

Now the Indian woman moves the three stones a little closer together and sets on them a big clay pot. This she fills with water, dipping from the water jar with a gourd ladle. While the water heats, she goes out to the porch to the millstone, where she grinds a handful of half-toasted corn into flour and sifts it through a horsehair sieve. Returning to the fire, she puts a little salt, lard, and a stalk of onion into the boiling water. Then she pours in the flour, stirring it with a wooden spoon

80

until it is dissolved. She peels a few potatoes, washes them in a dried half-pumpkin shell that serves as a basin, and adds them with a few cabbage leaves to the corn soup. When potatoes and cabbage are cooked, the thick soup, or *mazamorra*, is ready to eat.

The family gathers round the fire, sitting on the ground or on small wooden benches. The mother lifts the pot from the fire, fills the clay or gourd dishes with the steaming gruel, and passes them to her hungry family. The basket of toasted corn passes from hand to hand, and each eats what he likes. The bowls are filled a second time, and finally the father fills a dish for the dog and the cat, who have been waiting their turn patiently.

In the evening the Indian family sits for a while on the porch, and the father or one of the sons plays the flute or the panpipe (*rondador*). The sweet and melancholy notes of the Indian music are heard from first one house and then another. The shadows of the night slide down the mountainside. A crude kerosene lamp lights the hut with its reddish flame. The dogs bark at the night. Before long the lamp is blown out, and the family goes to sleep.

This is the way corn has been ground for hundreds of years, and this is the way it will be ground for years to come.

On three hearthstones over a fire of cornstalks, the iron pot or clay olla is placed to cook *mazamorra*, a thick smooth corn soup. The meal may lack variety but never lacks abundance.

With the day's work done, with stomach full and conscience at peace, it is good to enjoy a little music before lying down to rest.

Day is done. Mother and father are asleep within the house, but the sons roll out a rush mat and sleep on the adobe floor of the open porch.

COMMUNITY LIFE

CIVIL AFFAIRS

THE relation of the Otavalo Indians to the white-mestizo world around them has evolved slowly since the Spanish conquest into the definite pattern of political and social customs that prevail today. The Otavalo Indians have lived for centuries a life of civil obedience. Under the Inca Empire their life was controlled by indisputable law. The Spanish conquerors carried on this Inca pattern but with a new meaning. Whereas the Inca authority took the form of state benevolence, the Spanish authority came to mean social and economic enslavement. With stoic obedience the Andean Indian bowed to this exploitation, and today much of the colonial pattern is still in evidence.

There are three social classes in Ecuador today, generally called whites, mestizos, and Indians. Originally these represented racial distinctions—the conquering Spaniards and their descendants, the native Indians and their descendants, and the mestizos of mixed parentage. Today the racial composition is blended so that physical differences are not extreme, but the terms are still used to indicate social and cultural distinctions. "Whites" are those with some position, authority, wealth, or education, who wear modern European or North American style clothes. "Mestizos" or "*cholos*" are generally poorer, sometimes very poor, with little or no social position, who dress in the traditional old Spanish style, the men wearing cotton trousers and coats, the women long full skirts and shawls. "Indians" are those who still identify themselves with the old Indian cultures, who wear the Indian costumes, wear their hair long, or speak the Indian language instead of Spanish. Fortunately there exists no true race prejudice. The fact that any Indian, if he speaks Spanish, may become "mestizo" or even "white" simply by abandoning his community and changing his costume is an indication that the abuse of the Indian is not for his race but for the humble and resigned position associated with his clothes and culture.

Class or social discrimination, however, is still very real. In their dealings with whites and mestizos, Indians always face exploitation. Any white or mestizo be-

90

lieves himself entitled to take a "token" from an Indian—perhaps his broad-brimmed hat—and oblige him to work on private or public projects without pay. When whites or mestizos appear in the Indian communities, especially in those far from town, the Indians, hiding behind the fences, view the strangers with suspicion. Experience has taught that no good can come of such visits, for the Indians have been and are exploited without mercy; they have been and are kept in ignorance. Laws exist which would protect the Indians and condemn these abuses, but the authorities do not enforce them. Except for this abuse by petty authorities, the Indians are not in conflict with the government. They fear the law and try to comply with it, although it has for them little meaning.

The Indian continues in his obedience to the white man's world and yet survives by virtue of a subtle philosophy that is deep within him. He submits to humiliations without losing vitality in his Indian life. His intimate relations are with vast unchangeable values—mountains, rain, sun, and wind. His contact with these forces means far more to him than do calculated motivations such as characterize the white world. The exhaustion of carrying a burden over the mountains in obedience to a white man's wish does not touch the centers of his vitality; it does not humiliate him or affect his pride and sense of freedom as it would a white man's. Should the Indian find his mountains desecrated, his sacred lake destroyed, his ancestral earth taken from him, he would swiftly perish. But leave him his ancient pattern of plowing and harvesting, leave him his land and his primitive mysteries, and he can bear the heaviest yoke with dignity.

The Indian land around Otavalo is divided into "*parcialidades*," or communities. These are based on the titles given by the early Spaniards, for after the first decades of wholesale land seizure the Spanish monarchs instituted the policy of assigning lands to Indian communities. Title to land rested in the community as a whole; it could be divided among members of the community, as in practice it came to be, but could not be alienated from the community. To be sure, the most desirable valley lands had already been taken for Spanish haciendas, so that most of the Indian lands were on the steep mountainsides and hilltops. Over the years the Indians in the Otavalo region have regained some of the valley lands.

The various Indian communities are sharply divided by physical barriers. Those on the mountainside are divided by ravines and gravel washes; those

The Indians believe in order and peace. Violence must be dealt with by law. To hurt another is a crime, and the Commissioner of the Canton sees that the offenders are punished.

The guilty Indian is arrested and sentenced.

He must go to jail . . .

or do hours of public work in the market squares and streets of Otavalo.

lower in the valley, by streams and public roads, or one community may occupy a small hill. Some communities have more land than others, some better land than others; but, despite the unequal division, the traditional boundaries are preserved.

Each community has its alcalde, or mayor, elected in theory by the direct vote of the Indians but in practice appointed by the mayor of the parish to which the community belongs. Every year the parish mayor sponsors what in Ecuador are called "free elections," at which he appoints for each Indian community an Indian committee composed of president, vice-president, secretary, treasurer, and syndicate. Indians do not understand these names and call all members of the committee "mayors."

The Indian "mayors" receive no salary; they serve "patriotically." Their actual obligations, not those set forth in the law, consist of going from house to house naming workers needed by the parish mayor or some other public authority for public or private work. The Indians thus recruited may clean a public plaza, a street or road, or a private garden, orchard, or corral without receiving pay. Whenever the mayor, the sheriff, or the policeman of the parish town needs eggs, guinea pigs, or chickens, the Indian "mayor" receives the money and goes from house to house obliging the Indians to sell their products at the minimum price fixed by the parish authority. Very few Indians care to have these positions. Many refuse to accept them upon being appointed, because they lose time in the constant walking about from house to house and because the jobs will gain them enemies and the disapproval of other members of the community. Not without reason are the Indian officers accused of being lazy for passing "all the holy day" walking from house to house.

RELIGION

THE Indians' obedience to civil customs involves obedience to religious customs as well. When the Indians of the Otavalo region were conquered by the Incas, they were obliged to accept the Inca state religion of sun worship, but they were allowed to continue worshiping their own mysteries. The Spaniards adopted a similar attitude toward the Indians' acceptance of Catholicism. As long as the Indians confessed to be Christians and baptized their children in the church, the Catholic priests made no exclusive demands on their consciences. So the Otavalos today can be said to have a Catholic-pagan religion. They listen to Mass, not understanding it. They ask a favor of a saint with the same faith and hope that they worship Imbabura, their mountain. They have faith also in witch doctors, who with equal ease bring or prevent rain, make known a robber or other evildoer, indicate the hiding place of a lost object, or cure the sick. They fear the rainbow that pursues and violates the young girls; especially do they avoid waterfalls, because there a rainbow is always found. The occasional albino child born in the region, or the blue-eyed blond child of some Spanish landlord born to an Indian woman, is called the child of Father Imbabura.

The Indians, like many people, become more devout when there is some necessity or problem which they cannot themselves solve. In time of drought they pay for a Mass to the saints and also carry an offering to Father Imbabura. When the much-needed rain falls, it makes no difference which did them the favor, the saints or the mountain.

Sunday is the day for hearing Mass. Early in the morning the Indians leave their homes and pour over the hills into the towns. Like birds, they fill the streets in their bright ponchos and embroidered white blouses. Laughing and talking, they make their way to their favorite church. They enter, dip their fingers in the font of holy water, and piously make the sign of the cross. They kiss the feet of some saint who stands against the wall and then kneel on the floor or on a

bench. The Indian women sit in groups at the foot of the altars. While the priest celebrates Mass, they nurse their babies, letting the bigger children run around near by. The Indian children look at everything with big eyes, play together, and at times cry, making so much noise that the priest must send both mother and child out of the church. When priest or sacristan comes to collect the offering, the Indians faithfully add their coins. When Mass is over, they kiss the feet of the saint again, make the sign of the cross with holy water, and leave the church.

After Mass many Indians go to the tavern, ask for half a bottle of hard liquor—sugar-cane rum—and offer it to relatives and friends. The little cup, always full and spilling over, goes from hand to hand and mouth to mouth. The Indians drink with a delight, a pleasure apparent in all the muscles of the face. When the first half-bottle is emptied, someone asks for a second, then a third. Some Indian begins to play the flute or mouth organ, the panpipe or the guitar. The rest form a circle and dance, stamping loudly in perfect rhythm with the music, circling first one way then the other. The board floor of the tavern echoes like a drum beaten by the bare feet of the Indians. When the music stops, they sing their guttural songs over and over—"Hala-ha! Ha! Ha! Hala-ha! Ha! Ha!"—and the dance continues. The women watch the dancing, seated on the floor or on benches. From time to time they join in, either in the same circle or forming a separate one. When the husband drinks, the woman accepts only a little from time to time. One of the pair, more often the wife, must keep sober to look after the other and see that he gets home safely.

One by one the couples leave the tavern and begin the long walk home to their own communites. The drunken Indian staggers along with his head bent over his chest, unable to walk straight, almost falling at each step, muttering, exclaiming, and threatening with his fist. Only now when he is drunk does he feel himself the equal of any white. His wife walks beside him, supporting and urging him forward. So they walk through the streets of the town and reach the footpaths. Progress is slow and laborious. At last the drunken Indian cannot go any farther, and he falls heavily to the ground. There he sleeps in the road, sun or rain. His wife patiently sits beside him, watching and waiting for him to wake up so they can continue their journey.

Sunday is not only the day for Mass. It is also the day to see the world, to dance and sing, to meet one's friends in the village tavern.

Liquor makes dancing and laughter. But then it fills the heart with fury, drives you out into the road with its agony. There you sleep like the dead under the meager shade of the *maguey*, guarded by a friend or your faithful wife.

FIESTAS

FEAST days have ancient and profound meaning for the Indians. Fiestas are much more than just celebrations, though their primeval religious meanings have been lost and their aboriginal patterns confused and blended with Catholicism. Whatever they may appear to the white world, to the Indian the fiestas sum up the whole social order of his life. They divide the year and create a structure as orderly as the winter and summer seasons of the other latitudes.

Life in the high Andes is stern. Life is a continuous struggle of rigorous economy. The soil is shallow, the weather severe. Life is a tremendous burden that must be carried up and down precipitous trails. Life is breathed in the chilling thin air of nine and ten thousand feet. Life is working ceaselessly from dawn to dusk. Only the fiestas interrupt this tireless rhythm.

A fiesta is a wave of jubilance that pushes all before it. Flooding from the mountains, it washes into the valley, fills the streets of Otavalo with a surge of pagan energy. In singsong chant the Indians come running, their eyes fiery, their skin deep red, their nimble feet casting up clouds of summer dust. Intently they weave back and forth across the road following a pattern of some forgotten pilgrimage, till they join hundreds of other Indians who are playing flutes and dancing in circles through the town streets. The white world recedes before them, makes way for the tide of passion. Drunk as the gods, staggering with *chicha*, the Indians drink with a capacity and vigor unequaled in this world. Drinking, dancing, drinking, till they fall unconscious in the equatorial sun. Yet the drinking and dancing is no orgy of dissipation. It is rather a summoning-up of the violent energies of their life, an ecstasy and an exaltation.

Year after year the Indians celebrate their fiestas, spending their savings, consuming quantities of *chicha* and hard liquor, dancing often eight days at a time. The endurance of both the Indians and the mestizos who join the celebration is incredible. They are bothered neither by sun nor rain, by heat nor cold. They dance without resting, breathing thick clouds of dust raised by their pounding

100

feet. Day and night they dance and drink, to the tune of flute, panpipe, guitar, and tambourine, or perhaps to the music of a brass band of musicians from town.

The Catholic priests, who accompanied the Spanish conquerors and later the colonists, wisely made no attempt to block the Indian feast days. It is known that the priests were accustomed to organize fiestas in honor of saints of the Catholic calendar, supplanting or taking advantage of the dates of traditional pagan Indian festivals. The pagan ecstasy was simply converted to Christianity by the addition of a saint's day, a Mass, and a benediction. For the Otavalos the greatest festival of all comes in the last week of June, and June 24 is the day of the great Catholic saint, John the Baptist. So now in the name of San Juan the Indians sweep down from the hills, drink *chicha* for five days and nights, fill the air with their plaintive, haunting flutes, and dance and weep and fight.

The origin of the San Juan fiesta is unknown. There is little doubt that the Otavalo Indians celebrated it long before the coming of the Spaniards. The early chroniclers tell of a great native fiesta celebrated during the summer solstice. It is likely that the present San Juan festival is a continuation of this ancient pagan celebration.

No one knows what may have been the original meaning of the fiesta. It seems to have been a simulated or perhaps real battle between different groups of communities, each of which tried to take possession of the little plaza where the dances were to take place. These battles occurred up until a few years ago and resulted always in some dead and wounded. The community or group of allied communities which arrived first took possession of the little plaza and began the dances. Other communities or groups of them descended from the surrounding hills, entered the plaza, and fought with fists and even with knives to dislodge the firstcomers. Each group was surrounded by spectators who would shout directions and cheer the fighters on. When a fight had ended and a new attack was being planned, the dances continued in several circles. As they danced, the Indians sang and accompanied themselves with flutes and panpipes and conch shells and cattle horns. When the fight began again, the circles disintegrated, the dance was stopped, and everyone ran to take part in the struggle, insulting and threatening the "enemy" and bragging of his own courage and strength. When at last it was decided to put an end to this custom, considered savage by the whites, the police of Otavalo proved unable to keep order and had to be reinforced by police and soldiers from Ibarra, the next large town to the north.

The fiesta of San Luis Obispo
in the parish town of San Rafael

Today, in spite of the proscription against fighting, the fiesta goes on with the old enthusiasm. For three days the Indians celebrate in the little plaza of San Juan on the edge of Otavalo. Circles of dancers move around the plaza, dancing and dancing. The air is filled with singing, filled with the music of flutes, panpipes, mouth organs, guitars, and tambourines. Again and again they repeat the classic song:

Hala-ha! Ha! Ha!   Hala-ha! Ha! Ha!   Hala-ha! Ha! Ha!   Hala-ha! Ha! Ha!

And still they dance, circling first in one direction, then in the other, raising and stamping their feet with force and rhythm. Now again they poise threatening fists, trying to start a fight with an "enemy" group, for the Indians, animated with alcohol, scoff at the authorities. The white-mestizo population of Otavalo comes to watch the dancing. Booths are set up around the edge of the little plaza to sell taffy, cookies, potato patties, liquor, and *chicha*, and even a kind of sherbet made of ice brought all the way from the perpetual snow fields that top Mount Cotacachi.

During the three days of the festival the road from Otavalo to the San Juan plaza is full of people coming and going. The streets of Otavalo itself are gay with Indians dancing and singing as they pass back and forth from their homes. Every Indian who can afford it pays for the privilege of having a Mass said in honor of a cross or a saint, so the altars of the churches are filled with little statuettes of San Juan and with big wooden crosses adorned with ribbons and colored papers and five- and ten-sucre bills. These saints and crosses are taken home again with great ceremony and placed in a household shrine where they bring blessing to all who celebrate there.

Costumes worn for the San Juan festival have changed little in recent years. The general theme of the costuming seems to be imitation of whites. Well beforehand the Indians make the rounds of the houses in town looking for old shoes, leggings, caps, military hats and helmets, riding breeches, vests, and jackets, to rent or to buy. In late years sweaters and sun glasses have been bought in the stores. Besides these things the Indians have the seamstresses in town sew them special trousers of garish printed cloth. The costume is completed with a mask of cardboard or wire screen.

A favorite disguise is that of soldier; the costume usually requires only military cap and coat. *Mayordomos*, the managers of haciendas, are popular with leather chaps, vest, straw sombrero, spurs, and a long whip. Another costume which appears every year is the monkey or "little devil"; a full single-piece suit covers the body from head to foot with holes for the eyes and mouth and a tail behind.

Today not all the Indians of the district concentrate in Otavalo. The communities far from town celebrate the fiesta in some near-by place, where all neighboring groups gather. The Indians of the parish of Ilumán, four or five miles north of Otavalo, celebrate in their own community. The communities belonging to the parishes of San Rafael, González Suárez, and San Pablo, on the eastern and southern sides of Lake San Pablo, celebrate San Juan together in the open plaza of Araque near the shores of the lake. The Indians of these communities prefer to dress as *mayordomos* with wide chaps. Over the shoulder they wear a hide sewn with many bronze bells of various sizes. At each step the bells sound, following the rhythm of the dance. These same Indians play flutes more than a yard long and dance carrying a pole horizontally across their shoulders. A few disguise themselves as women, using the beautifully embroidered blouses of their wives.

The festival of San Luis Obispo, the nineteenth of August, is perhaps better organized and more elaborate than that of San Juan. Some years ago this fiesta took place in Otavalo, but now it is celebrated only in the parish of San Rafael, a small town overlooking Lake San Pablo. The old people tell how one of the priests of San Rafael, desperate with the poor income of his parish and realizing that this was due to the fact that the Indians celebrated all their fiestas not at home but in Otavalo, decided to persuade them to spend their money in San Rafael instead. He asked a sculptor to make a statue of San Luis Obispo. One day an Indian passing behind the church discovered near the old walls of the convent the figure of San Luis. The news spread through the community, and soon most of the people were in the plaza telling each other varied and fantastic versions of the miraculous apparition of the saint. Then the priest came out and invited the people into the church. Climbing to the pulpit, he thanked Heaven for its divine favor for turning toward San Rafael and bringing a miracle to pass there. He made the people understand that if San Luis had appeared in San Rafael it was because he wanted his day celebrated there. Since then the fiesta

105

has in fact been celebrated there, and the parish, once poor, is now rich and sought after by many priests.

The fiesta of San Luis is sponsored by eight or ten patrons who are called *corazas*. Each patron is accompanied by two Indians disguised as *yumbos*, savage Indians from the Amazon jungles, and by a *loa*, or praise-maker. The costume of the sponsor is most elaborate and elegant. It consists of trousers and a long full blouse of fine cloth decorated with lace, spangles, and sequins; white stockings; sandals tied with ribbons; and a hat in the shape of an inverted half-moon, its upper border filled with colored plumes, its lower border edged with rented earrings of gold and precious stones. This costume, particularly the hat, is worth several thousand sucres. The patron assigns his best friend to watch over it, and this guard follows him like a shadow throughout the celebration of the fiesta. The patron himself does not drink so that he will run no risk of losing any of the jewels. The *yumbos* wear red or blue trousers and blouse adorned with a few spangles, stockings, sandals, and a crown of cardboard decorated along its upper edge with colored plumes. The praise-maker, who is usually white or mestizo, wears a costume like that of the patron but without jewels.

The patrons, the *yumbos*, and the praise-makers all make arrangements with women of the town of San Rafael to prepare their costumes for the fiesta. On the night before the fiesta, each patron goes to the house of the woman responsible for his costume to have his hair dressed. He is given a kind of permanent wave, his hair moistened with *chicha* and wound into curls with strips of old cloth. He brings the hairdresser a gift. On the fiesta day all come to be dressed in their costumes, to have their faces painted white and circles of red put on their cheeks.

In full costume the patron, sometimes on horseback, sometimes on foot, passes through the town followed by his *yumbos* and his praise-maker. The group is preceded by an Indian band, three musicians playing small panpipes and one playing the tambourine. Before the fiesta Mass the patron and his companions make an official entrance led by the town band of San Rafael playing a special song for this holiday. They circle the plaza and enter the church to sit ceremoniously on chairs at one side of the main altar. The band leaves to bring in another patron and his party, till all the patrons have arrived, each led by the band in his turn. The plaza and the streets of the town are full of Indians. From all sides the panpipes and tambourines of the native bands are heard. The music, sweet and melancholy, evokes a past grandeur.

106

When the Mass is over, the patrons leave one by one, while the plaza echoes to the deafening sound of firecrackers and rockets. Some of the patrons carry two long chains of old silver attached to their waists and stringing far behind, held up throughout their length by relatives and friends. The patron walks with a slow and dignified step, holding in his right hand a scepter adorned with flowers and ribbons. His face is almost completely hidden by the jewels hanging from the brim of the hat. His guard shades him with an umbrella. The praise-maker walks with him, and the *yumbos* flank the pair on either side.

Changing his hat for one of felt with brim turned up in front, decorated with spangles and sequins, the patron climbs on a horse covered with a large colored mantle. The praise-makers and the *yumbos* mount other similarly decorated horses, and all begin to gallop around the plaza. They approach the atrium of the church, and here the praise-maker gives his discourse, praising the patron, who has spared no effort to honor the fiesta of San Luis, praising the goodness and holiness of the parish priest, praising the honesty and enthusiasm of the parish mayor, and ending with *"Viva's!"* for each of these people, for the gathering, and for himself. At once the patron sets off at a gallop, followed closely by the praise-maker and the *yumbos*, who hurl candy or bits of brown sugar trying to hit his face and draw blood. The patron may defend himself only by leaving his pursuers behind or by ducking his head. He may not cover his face with his hands, and he has no candy or sugar to throw back. From the plaza the party goes to a tavern, then to the house of the patron where the fiesta continues for several days.

Patron of the San Luis fiesta

Crosses and saints from distant communities are carried to town for the blessing of a fiesta Mass.

Indians who are not dancing or playing flutes stand by the hour in their brilliant
ponchos watching the fiesta throng.

In front of the community chapel Indians in outlandish costume of white people, soldiers, and hacienda owners dance the monotonous San Juan fiesta dance, moving in a circle, playing flutes, stamping, and shouting.

There are traditional places to celebrate the San Juan fiesta, like this broad plaza at the foot of Mount Imbabura.

Soft birdlike tunes are played again
and again on the flutes.

San Juan fiesta is the occasion to
masquerade and to clown.

From morning till night, drunk or
sober, the Indians sway and stamp
to the rhythm of song, flute, or
mouth organ.

All night long for five nights masqueraded dancers drift from house to house, drinking *chicha* and eating *mote*—boiled kernels of newly ripened corn and beans.

Chicha, the old Indian drink of fermented corn, makes men laugh and sing.

But *aguardiente*, the distilled fire-water rum, makes men weep and fight. Ancient rivalries flare into bloody blows. Time turns back; the Indians fight as if for traditional leadership of the valley.

CO-OPERATION

HOUSEBUILDING is a grand occasion. It is an expression of the co-operative spirit whereby the close-knit Indian community makes short work of a task too time-consuming for an individual farmer and a festive social affair of an essentially tedious hard job. It is also a great moment in an Indian's life, a harvest of his labors, a gesture of prestige and well-being.

If an Indian is planning a simple old-style house of wattle and thatch, all the materials can be gathered on the mountain, and with the help of friends and relatives the construction can be completed in a day. But if he is building a modern Indian house with tamped-earth walls and tile roof, construction is more complex. The earthen wall must be built slowly, for each layer of wall must dry before the next is laid. The walls are built under the direction of a master wall-builder, an Indian specializing in this construction, for it takes great skill and a trained eye. Only a few people at a time are needed to help the professional wall-builder. It is for the final job of putting on the tile roof that the whole community comes together in fiesta spirit.

In a clearing under the eucalyptus trees the rectangular shell of the house stands drying and settling for several months. Its massive earthen walls are two feet thick, smooth and hard as cement. The surface shows the shape of the wooden mold in which damp earth was packed and tamped down, shows how the mold was moved and the tamping repeated to follow round the base of the wall, and how a second layer was built on top, and perhaps a third where the walls are highest under the peak of the roof.

On the day set for the roofing the host has been up since starlight working with his family to prepare quantities of food and drink for his hard-working guests. Around the half-constructed house lie the piles of materials he has collected—stacks of red tiles, great loops of *cabuya* fiber, roof poles, and timbers.

Everyone has been invited. Many have been up since long before daybreak to

116

Housebuilding is too large a job for a single family, so the Indians organize a community work-party.

finish their daily tasks early so they can work all day long on the roofing. The sun is just rising above the mountain when the guests begin to arrive. The men come with spades or hoes, or a few tiles as a gift, or a few sucres to help out the host. The women come in a line carrying great ollas of *chicha* as presents. Indians gather from up on the mountain, from down in the valley. From all over the community they come to finish the new house. Soon the quiet hillside is turned into a beehive of activity. Heavy blue and red ponchos are thrown on the ground, and the keen morning air is filled with calls and laughter as the Indians swarm around the new building. Each knows his task from long experience, and the roofing progresses swiftly.

The hewn wooden pillars of the porch are set in place. Two massive beams of eucalyptus wood are raised to position on top of the earthen walls. Upon these beams the rafters of the roof are nailed, secured overhead to a roof beam of slender eucalyptus wood. The roof is taking shape, sloping down over the porch. The Indians hop about the structure like birds, lashing slender saplings of eucalyptus across the rafters with *cabuya* fiber. On top of these saplings they lash long green canes to form a solid base, and the roof is ready for tiling.

Now the master mason takes over. He is a mestizo and, like the master wall-builder, works for a salary. Now the pattern of activity shifts as to a new figure in a dance. People are running here, running there, digging, hauling water, chopping up the earth to mix a smooth adobe mortar. Now the Indians form a line from the piled tiles to the workers on the roof. From hand to hand the tiles pass, flowing upward to the master mason, who lays them accurately along the roof beam and down along the eaves. Once these key tiles are set, the rest of the roof is tiled by the Indians.

In the midst of all the activity the owner of the house, a true host, rushes back and forth among the workers with gourds of *chicha*, pressing the fiery drink on his guests till spirits run wild in shouts and jokes and laughter. From the kitchen there flows a continuous round of *mazamorra* soup and hominy and parched corn—as much as the workers can eat. Everyone works faster and faster, each competing with his neighbor to see how many tiles he can lay. Passers-by are drawn into the activities with jokes and threats or bombardments of mud from the rooftop. The host hurries out to offer *chicha* to the newcomer. Few refuse to help in the building. No one is obliged to offer his help, but the Indians understand the mutual advantage of co-operation. Someday community aid will be

118

necessary for each of them, and the Indian who helps expects to be helped in his turn.

Thus the housebuilding is more than a task: It soon becomes a lively party. There is a contagious excitement and joy which each worker feels as if the house were his own. Everyone works hard, taking delight in the fine red tiles and pride in the excellent carpentering of the beams. In co-operativeness and sociability, the strength and unity of the Indian community is forged.

The work may be finished in a day, or it may take two or three. When all the tiles are laid, the women move the kitchen into the new house and make more soup and hominy. And the party continues in a deluge of good food and *chicha*, with dancing to the plaintive flutes and panpipes, till utter exhaustion brings the festivities to a close.

Guests arrive in a festive mood, ready for work and play. They swarm over the roof, lashing down the rafters, making ready for the roof tiles.

The brackets for the eaves are expertly nailed in place. Everyone knows his task, and the work proceeds swiftly.

All work with the best of will. They joke and tease, throw mud at each other, eat quantities of *mazamorra* soup, and drink endless gourdfuls of *chicha*.

Under the direction of the master-mason the first tiles of the ridgepole are laid in position.

Tiles are passed upward in a steady line and laid quickly on the cane roof, held in place with a bit of adobe mortar.

A new home and a secure future before her eyes, the Indian mother sees her house completed.

Housebuilding is
a grand occasion.

PRESTIGE

SOCIAL standing is not easily apparent among the Otavalo Indians. Whether a family is rich or poor, they wear essentially the same clothes, live in the same type of house, do the same sort of work as their neighbors. Nevertheless, there is ambition and vanity, and Indians who have been successful want recognition. To gain position and respect from money, the Indian must spend money, and the recognized way to spend money is to sponsor a fiesta. This gesture of generosity to all the community brings a man honor; it is a sure way to gain or maintain prestige. Social pressure has made it the most important social obligation of a man's life. The Indian struggles to accumulate enough money—even if he must steal it—to sponsor a fiesta himself. For until he has done so he is not considered a responsible member of the community; it is as if he were still a boy. The most humiliating insult for an Indian is to be told, "You are a poor man—you have not yet sponsored a fiesta!" Only the hopelessly poor can resign themselves to the disgrace of such a failure.

Essentially a reception in honor of the host, the privately sponsored fiesta is a formal, elaborate, and expensive affair known as the *paso del cargo*, "passing the burden," or sharing the obligation. Nothing is known of the origin of the name or the pattern of the celebration. The principal sponsor is called the

124

"Captain" and spends a minimum of two thousand sucres (roughly $150). A close friend who assists him in the role of "Page" spends at least another fifteen hundred sucres. As this represents many years' saving, even for a successful Indian, the *paso del cargo* may indeed be a "burden."

The sponsors start the three-day fiesta by buying a Mass, complete with brass band and firecrackers, for the patron saint of the community, who is carried to Otavalo to receive the blessings of the service. On the appointed day the sponsors and their guests gather at the community chapel. The doors are opened, and the party files into the cold interior to gather around the altar where rests the patron saint, splendid in gilt beads, paper flowers, and Spanish lace. Reverently they lift the saint from her pedestal and carry her forth from the chapel. Outside the procession is met with a fusillade of firecrackers and the blaring music of a band of musicians hired from town. They strike up a spirited Ecuadorian tune, and the cortege starts for town. Half-dancing, half-running, the party descends the precipitous footpaths to the valley below.

The sponsors have paid dearly for the Mass; it is long and stately. Within the shadowed church the Indians kneel in silence, their faces awed with the magic of the ceremony, the chanting of the priest, the sweet odor of the censer, the tingling altar bells. They cross themselves, mumbling now and again responses that hold for them no meaning.

With shining faces they leave the service, carrying their saint with them. Their spirits overflowing, the party hurries down the street to the nearest tavern, for now it is time to celebrate, to drink in honor of their saint and their good host. The saint is elevated to a safe place on a table where she can best participate in the festivities. And the drinking and the dancing go on to the half-gay, half-mournful music of the band.

On the second day the dancing and drinking continues at the homes of the Captain and his assistant, the Page. On the third day the parties reach their highest pitch. The brass band plays on its endless *sanjuanitos*, the popular Ecuadorian songs of mixed European and Indian origin. Each piece lasts scarcely a minute and costs the host one sucre. Everyone is drinking *chicha*, and with each round of music the guests prance and stamp in a circle. Some wear costumes, masks, and gaudy pantaloons similar to the costumes of the San Juan fiesta, but most of the guests are dressed simply in their best ponchos, their newest shirts and blouses. Another round of music ends. Bowls of steaming *mazamorra*

125

soup are passed from the kitchen. The guests pause in their dancing to eat and drink again.

More and more friends and relatives come to honor the party. In the morning they arrive in a long single file, men then women, bearing gifts for the Captain —money, or food such as salt, bread, fruit, and *chicha*. The Captain awaits his guests at the entrance of his dooryard, thanks each for his present, and offers them with his own hand a bowl of *chicha* and a bowl of *mazamorra* soup. Other members of the community are gathered at the home of the Page, where a similar party is in progress, and the band is kept busy hustling between the two houses to play serenades.

At noon of the third day the final ceremony of the fiesta begins. Mounted on horseback, the Page leaves his house, followed by his court of friends and relatives, and rides over the fields to the home of the Captain. He rides with the splendor of a potentate. From head to foot he glistens in a gaudy suit of pink and blue, sparkling with designs of silver paper, resplendent with plumes of crimson feathers. The Captain, adorned in a similar costume of brilliant elegance, also mounts a horse and awaits the arrival of his assistant. Beside him on a third mount sits the little *loa*, or praise-maker, a boy of eight or ten, dressed as gaily as the older sponsors. His eyes sparkle with excitement, but he sits on his horse with calm self-possession. The two courts meet with dignity. The Captain leans over and kisses the cheek of the Page. The little praise-maker recites a poem in honor of the occasion, but his piping voice is lost in the hubbub and laughter. And the band plays again as bowls and gourds of *chicha* are passed from hand to hand.

Now the Captain, the Page, and the praise-maker ride forth from the dooryard of the Captain's home, followed by the band and the dancing guests. In a slow procession they serpentine down the mountainside to the plaza of the community chapel. Rockets and firecrackers explode. Little cannons go off like thunder. The band croaks and blares as the court reaches the chapel in clouds of pungent powder smoke. The plaza fills with Indians while the fireworks continue. The Captain, the Page, and the praise-maker separate. Each is surrounded by groups of relatives and friends who vie to offer a cup of liquor or more *chicha*. With great dignity the principals accept these manifestations of appreciation and homage. There is no doubt that they are the soul of the fiesta and that "sharing the obligation" brings them great prestige.

126

The Captain dismounts and, followed by the Page, the praise-maker, and the rest of the company, enters the church. One after another they mount the altar, kiss the mantle and feet of the saint, then leave. Dancing continues in the little plaza. When night begins to fall, the fiesta ends with the raising of a high and slender eucalyptus tree freshly stripped of its bark. At the top of the pole is fastened a platform loaded with money, bread, fruit, and other articles of food and clothing. Children and adults try to climb the slippery pole. They organize groups to help each other, slide, slip, and fall. The spectators, among them the curious from near-by towns, laugh with pleasure. Finally someone reaches the platform and, while the crowd shouts, takes possession of the booty.

This three-day ceremony is only the first half of "sharing the obligation." Captain and Page must at once name a date for a second and identical three-day celebration to be held three or four months later. During these intervening months the sponsors of the fiesta retain their titles of "Captain" and "Page." Only after the second part is completed have they fulfilled their obligation of sponsoring a fiesta.

Festivities begin in a church in Otavalo with a Mass and a blessing to the patron saint of the community to which the sponsor belongs. Right after Mass the party proceeds to revelry and drinking as the Indians dance and sing in the nearest tavern. Dancing continues all the way home to the community chapel, where the saint is returned to her altar.

For three days festivities continue at the home of the host, or Captain, of the fiesta. All the friends and relatives come bearing gifts—*chicha*, salt, bread, fruit, and presents of money—for a fiesta costs thousands of sucres, and all are anxious to help.

The guests are greeted by the Captain with bowls of *chicha* as they enter the dooryard. He toasts them one and all, and a merry time begins.

Chicha,
music, and
dancing

Black powder, earth, and rocks are jammed into heavy brass mortars that explode like tiny volcanoes, belching flame and smoke.

In their ornate costumes, the Captain, the Page, and a small boy known as the *loa* are the central figures around whom the ceremonies revolve. Toasts are drunk to all three, and the boy recites a poem.

Now all the party follow the leaders to the plaza of the community, dancing and singing as they trail down the hill.

Here the gallant procession disperses. Some continue dancing. Some enter the humble chapel to kiss the feet of the saint.

The Captain still sits on his horse like a king, but the end is coming soon. Bottle after bottle of *aguardiente* rum is passed around among the guests. Its lethal spirits overcome the Captain at last. He sinks to the ground in his splendid clothes and falls asleep. The fiesta is over.

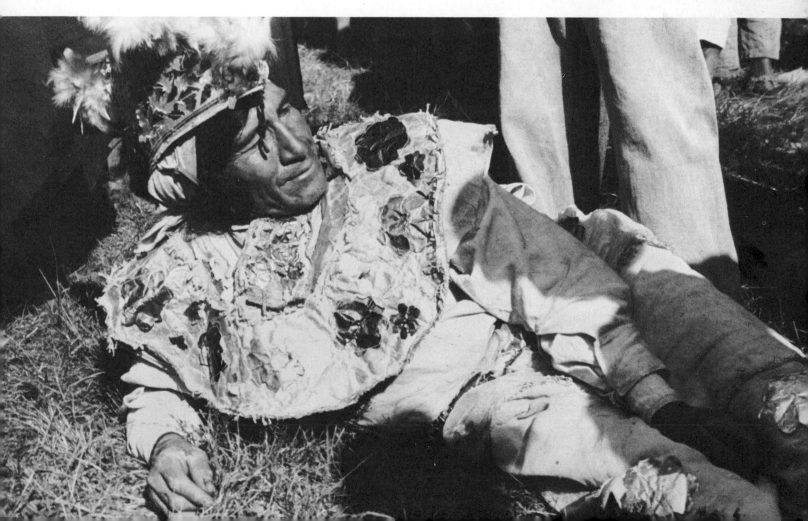

MARRIAGE

MARRIAGE is an elaborate rite, a community affair as imposing as the privately sponsored fiesta in its ceremony, costliness, and significance. Some years ago the majority of marriages were arranged by the parents. The betrothed couple, sometimes as young as twelve years, were ignorant of the affair until the day of the ceremony. Often the young people had not known each other before. Today most of the marriages, especially in communities close to the towns, are between boys and girls of eighteen years or so and follow a brief and simple courtship.

Usually the Indian boy becomes interested in the daughter of a neighbor or of a close friend of the family whom he has seen frequently. He follows the girl at a prudent distance whenever the opportunity presents itself. At first he does nothing but follow, letting the girl know indirectly that he is interested in her. Then one of these times, hiding behind a wall or a tree, he throws a few bits of earth or stones at her. Later he speaks to her, teasing, but still keeping his distance. Finally, he comes close and struggles with her to get her *fachalina*, the cloth she wears on her head. The girl fights with all her might to keep it. If she has decided to accept her suitor, she ends by letting him take the *fachalina*. If not, she will not give it up.

The boy who has obtained the headcloth and with it the consent of his sweetheart tells his parents that he has chosen a wife. His parents visit the girl's family and discuss with her parents the conditions and circumstances of the projected marriage. An agreement reached, the parents of the boy return after a few days with a bowl of cooked potatoes, eggs, guinea pigs, and chickens and a bottle of liquor for the family of the bride. After presenting twelve such gifts as this and after inviting the family of the bride several times to a tavern, the ceremony called "placing the rosary" takes place. The mayor of the Indian community hangs a long rosary of corals, copper beads, old silver coins, and an enormous crucifix of silver first around the neck of the bride and then of the bridegroom while the two kneel facing him. The mayor blesses the couple. The father of the bride blesses the bridegroom, and the father of the bridegroom blesses the bride. In pre-Columbian times this, or a variation of it, was probably part or all of the marriage ceremony. Even today the Indians consider themselves legally married after the placing of the rosary, and the couple live together as man and wife.

Some time later the couple go to the office of the civil registry, where they are married according to the law of the Republic of Ecuador. The Indians attach little importance to this ceremony. They do not celebrate it; they merely comply with the law to avoid complications or punishment. Finally, after another period of time varying from a month to a year the religious marriage takes place. For both the civil and the religious marriages two witnesses are needed. Since most Indians are illiterate, these witnesses are usually whites who sign the register declaring that they know the couple—a service for which they are paid one or two sucres. For the religious marriage there must be sponsors, corresponding to best man and maid of honor. Generally the sponsors are Indians, perhaps the parents of one of the couple. When the marriage has been inscribed on the church register, when the witnesses have signed, when the priest has been paid his fifty sucres and the sacristan his five, the bridal pair accompanied by the sponsors and relatives enter the church and kneel at the foot of the main altar. Bride and groom, each holding a candle, are wrapped in a veil which covers both their heads while the priest celebrates the Mass. When the Mass is over and the party is outside the church, the couple gratefully kiss the hands of their sponsors.

The wedding party spends a while drinking in a tavern. From there they go to the house of the bridegroom to continue drinking *chicha* and liquor and to eat hominy and *mazamorra* soup with guinea pig. At the end of the day the sponsors take the bride and groom to a room and lock them in with a padlock. Outside the dance continues. Cups of liquor and bowls of *chicha* liven humors and quench thirst. The harp, indispensable for wedding music, is played by two musicians, one plucking the cords, the other beating the sounding board like a drum. Guitars, flutes, and tambourines complete the orchestra. Rockets are fired off, frightening the dogs who run and bark. The ground echoes under the bare feet of the dancing Indians. So they pass all the night.

Next morning relatives and friends of the community arrive, each bringing a chicken, a guinea pig, eggs, salt, potatoes, *chicha*, liquor, or money. The gifts are turned over to the father of the bridegroom, who thanks each guest and personally offers him a bowl of *chicha* to drink and a bowl of *mazamorra* soup with guinea pig. A specially designated Indian takes charge of the gifts of food and distributes them to be cooked and served to the party. At noon the Indians go, still dancing, to the room where the bridal couple has been locked up. Harp, guitar, and flute serenade the couple. The sponsor opens the door, and everyone pours inside, crying, "Here we come, everybody!" "Take care you are not kissing her!" "Don't be embracing her—you had all night for that!" Everyone laughs and enjoys the teasing. Indians chosen to serve as waiters bring big pails of cinnamon water, made by boiling cinnamon a few minutes in water and adding liquor and sugar, with bits of biscuit and bread scattered in it. The cups are filled with the cinnamon water and bread and passed first to the bridal pair, then to the rest of the company. Coming out into the dooryard, the couple dances in a circle with all the guests. Those who get drunk are promptly led to a separate room and locked up there. When they get over their drunkenness, they sally forth again to join the festivities. In this way the Indians avoid quarrels and scandals.

After the dance of the bride and groom everyone goes to the house of the bride, where the traditional lunch appropriate for marriages—*mazamorra* soup with guinea pig—is served. Immediately after lunch all go down to the brook for the ceremony called *ñavi mayllay*, "washing the face." The sponsors take a little water in a washbasin or wooden trough, sprinkle the petals of carnations and roses in it and, aided by the groom, wash the face, the arms, and the legs of the bride, advising her meanwhile to be a good wife. The water is changed, fresh flower petals are put in it, and the sponsors with the help of the bride wash the face, arms, and legs of the groom, counseling him to be a good husband. After this ceremony the waiters arrange a table in the field, spreading head-cloths on the ground and placing on them quantities of toasted corn, boiled peas, beans, hominy, potatoes, and cheese. Everyone sits around this table eating and talking. The waiters make the rounds with *chicha* and liquor. Returning to the house of the bride, the party continues dancing and drinking. On the third day the celebration takes place in the house of the sponsors. Often it continues for eight or ten days, passing from one house to another.

142

BAPTISM

ALL Indian children are baptized in the church and are given names from the calendar of saints. Most popular names for boys are "Juan," "Pedro," "Manuel," "Miguel," "José," and "Andrés"; for girls, "María," "Rosa," "Juana," "Carmen," "Manuela," and "Dolores."

On the day after birth, or at the latest on the fifth day, the father, accompanied by several relatives, brings the baby to the house of the friend he has chosen as *compadre*, or godfather. Since this relationship calls for mutual help and confidence, the Indian usually chooses a white man who can assist him in case of difficulties with the law. Every Indian has some white friend or business acquaintance who will be ready to stand as godfather to his child. The Indian father brings a gift of a chicken, eggs, bread, and fruit and asks his friend to do him the honor of holding the baby for baptism. The godfather accepts the gifts. He asks if the father has the birth certificate from the civil registry, and, if this is ready, the godfather arranges the hour of the baptism with the priest. This done, the godfather buys the baby a ready-made shirt of cheap Ecuadorian cloth sold for this purpose in the stores and a big kerchief of yellow, red, or blue. As soon as the godfather presents his gift of clothes, the baby is dressed in them. Then the baby is taken to the church for the Catholic baptism ceremony.

If the parish priest needs workers to cut or carry wood, to weed or cultivate the garden, or to sweep the church or convent, he exacts this service in exchange for the baptism and in advance of it. When no work is needed, the priest is paid in money by the godfather. In either case the godfather pays the sacristan. After the baptism the Indians thank the godfather, kiss his hand, and return to their home community. Sometimes they will go first to the house of the godfather, where each is given a little cup of liquor. Occasionally, godfathers of baptism

143

are Indians, and in this case the party on leaving the church goes to a tavern, drinks a quantity of liquor, and returns home to continue drinking and dancing.

Exactly one month after the baptism, father, mother, and baby, accompanied by relatives and friends, come to the house of the godfather with another gift similar to the first to "introduce the baby to his godfather." The godfather serves cups of liquor, and the Indians address all members of the godfather's family as *compadres*, godfathers, or *comadres*, godmothers. When the Indians say goodbye, they kiss the hand of each member of the godfather's family.

SICKNESS

FOR the Indian, sickness is a struggle with evil spirits. Only the Indian *brujo*, or witch doctor, can drive the spirits from the patient. The *brujo* usually begins his career as apprentice to an established witch doctor. Frequently the office passes from father to son. The profession is not confined to one sex; both men and women practice witchcraft and gain equal prestige. The activities of the *brujo* are various. He may as easily cure a sick person or make a healthy one ill. He may bring or send away the rains, identify a robber, indicate the place where a lost article may be found, cause one to love, another to hate, make tyrants kind, and vice versa. The Indians in general believe that the best *brujos* live in the tropical jungle of the Amazon and in Santo Domingo de los Colorados, a jungle valley west of Quito. For this reason a *brujo* of the Otavalos who wishes to perfect his knowledge and gain greater prestige must spend some time in one or the other of these jungle regions.

The *brujo* does not exercise his calling all the time, nor does he expect to earn his living from it. His activities as witch doctor take place at night, perhaps two or three times a week. The rest of the time he is an Indian like any other; he works and amuses himself with the rest.

Although he has many functions, the *brujo*'s chief importance is as the doctor. The Indians come to him in full confidence whenever they are ill. Their belief concerning the cause of sickness is one that is widespread among primitive people—the belief that some foreign object has entered the body. If this foreign body —a splinter, lizard, beetle or other insect—can be extracted, the sickness will disappear. This reasoning is logical and convincing to the Indian, for the sick man can see the cause of his illness removed before his eyes. The *brujo* must first determine the nature of the disease that is troubling the patient. He rubs the body of the patient with a candle and then examines the candle long and carefully, for on its surface as in an X-ray appears the cause of illness. The disease is spread throughout the body; it must be brought to a head, so the *brujo*

145

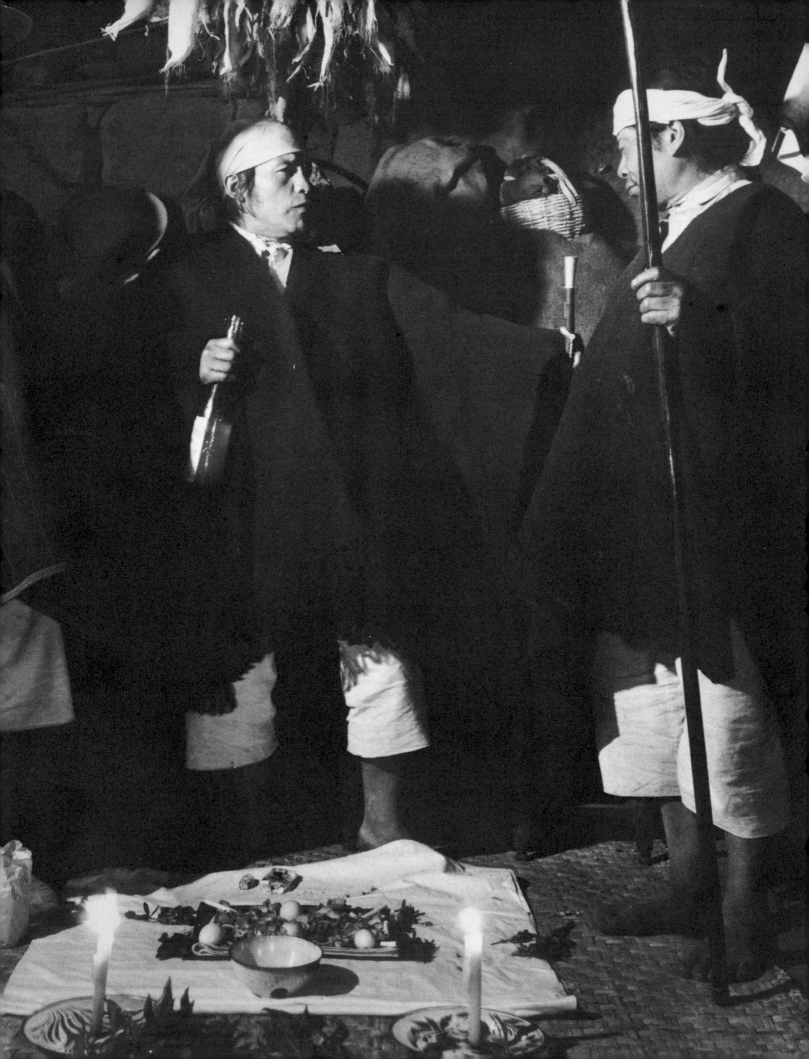

rubs the patient with branches of medicinal herbs to draw the illness to one place. Once the disease has been diagnosed and localized, it remains only to extract the cause of the sickness. This may be done by sucking the area of concentration and producing before the astonished patient a frog or lizard. The *brujo* may also rub the infected area with eggs which absorb the disease; the eggs turn black, the absorbed poison making them so hard, the Indians say, that they cannot be broken even against a stone. This basic treatment is accompanied by elaborate and mysterious ceremonies to impress the patient.

The sick man arrives at the home of the *brujo* with all the articles needed for the treatment: a bottle of liquor, cigarettes, matches, candles, eggs, red roses, carnations, and medicinal herbs from the mountain. The *brujo*, wearing a large red poncho, his head tied up in a varicolored silk handkerchief, begins the treatment by arranging a table or altar on the mud floor of the house. On a straw mat he lays a pattern of magic amulets. First he spreads out a woman's headcloth, strews roses and carnations on it, and places on each corner an egg, herbs, and cigarettes. In front of the cloth he sets two candles on china plates with the liquor, a large china cup, and a spoon between them. Beyond these he spreads more sprays of medicinal herbs.

The *brujo* sits behind this altar. On his right is the helper. At his left sits the patient, his head wrapped up in a white handkerchief, his left hand holding a spear so that evil spirits will see that he is well armed and will stay away from him. The *brujo* lights the candles and a small quantity of liquor that has been placed in the cup. All three—the *brujo*, the helper, and the patient—then light up cigarettes. The *brujo* blows smoke from his cigarette in big gulps, one after the other, producing a noise like a strong wind and invoking the blessings of the *brujos* of Santo Domingo de los Colorados, the power of the mountains and of the waterfalls. Then he takes a mouthful of liquor and blows it in a fine spray at the candles. The vapor flames as it passes over the lighted candles. The room seems filled with blue fire. The *brujo* goes on with his exorcisms, brandishing in his right hand first the bottle of liquor and then a wooden wand adorned with copper rings. With great puffs he continues blowing clouds of liquor and cigarette smoke at the candles and over the head of the sick man, who sits there motionless, clutching the spear. The conjuring grows more intense. Suddenly the *brujo* leans forward, seizes two of the eggs, and rubs them over the back and chest of the sick man. The illness is absorbed into the eggs.

147

The treatment is over, and the *brujo* ceremoniously clears the altar. He blows out another cloud of smoke and liquor as he moves the bottle or the wand in a circle over the cloth and blesses the altar, making the sign of the cross with his hand. He folds the altar cloth, taking care that all the flower petals remain inside. The helper takes the herbs and eggs and throws them far away into the night—they are charged with the disease that has been conjured from the sick man. The folded altar cloth is given to the patient. He is told that he must sleep upon it all that night to insure success of the treatment.

The patient now thinks he is well. His improvement has been immediate. His face no longer reflects pain and worry; he is smiling and tranquil. He thanks the *brujo*, pays him the fifteen or twenty sucres agreed upon beforehand, and starts for home. Not only the Indians but white people as well have faith in the *brujos*. When a *brujo* acquires fame, his patients come from all parts of Ecuador. There are stories told of *brujos* who have restored health to sick people given up by the best doctors and of rich aristocratic clients who have rewarded *brujos* with generous gifts, publicly proclaiming their gratitude.

Such faith do the Indians have in their *brujos* that they never consider the *brujo*'s actions in the light of reason. The simplest trick fools the most intelligent Indian. When a *brujo*, for example, undertakes to divine the author of a robbery or the place where a lost article may be found, he leaves his client inside the house, goes out on the porch of the house, and in a disguised voice tells who is to blame or where the lost object is to be found. The client supposes he has heard the *brujo* talking with a goblin or some other spirit.

The *brujos* know how to prepare potions to cause love, hate, pity, or to drive a man crazy. Impartial and disinterested practitioners, they administer according to the needs of their clients. Not long ago a Spanish landlord barely escaped death from a potion administered by his Indian cook; the peons of the hacienda, tired of the landlord's harsh treatment, got the potion from a *brujo* in order to make the landlord milder. In another such case the owner of a flour-mill went temporarily mad from eating a poisoned melon given him by an Indian. The poisoner readily confessed, but explained that he was only trying to make the miller, who had always been evil-tempered, a happier man.

The mystical relationships the Indians feel with the sun, the rain, and the earth, and the powers of good and evil, all make the *brujo* an important person in the community. His powers are respected by everyone.

148

The *brujo* blesses his altar of magic. The treatment is finished; the patient already feels relief from the evil spirits that have been causing his illness.

DEATH

THE Indian accepts death with a quiet resignation. His feelings are profound. He believes in the immortality of the soul, and he honors the deceased with a funeral of simple dignity. The death of a child has a significance different from that of a death of an adult. The Indian believes that if a dead child has been baptized, it becomes an angel and goes directly to heaven. The death of a baptized child is, then, not a reason for grief but for rejoicing. Those relatives and friends remaining on earth now have someone to intercede for them in heaven, helping them gain paradise in their turn. The body of the dead child is seated, as if living, upon a table or improvised platform, and the corpse is held in position by cords. An arch of branches and flowers frames the body. Candles burn on either side.

The relatives and friends of the deceased gather in the house of death. While watching over the corpse, they drink *chicha* and liquor and dance to the music of a flute or panpipe. On the second or third day the corpse is placed in a wooden coffin and buried in the cemetery of the nearest town. Returning from the cemetery, the funeral party enters a tavern and drinks once more before each person returns to his home.

The death of an adult is cause for sorrow. The nearest relatives weep inconsolably. The corpse is undressed and bathed with water in which has been boiled a number of herbs which are said to have the property of preserving the body temporarily. The body is then dressed in its best clothes and placed in a coffin, as soon as one can be brought from town. The coffin, which is usually painted a bright orange, rests on a table or platform, a candle burning at each corner. Relatives and friends sit on benches or on the ground against the walls of the porch and house. *Chicha* and liquor are passed constantly. The mourners drink, converse, and pray; they may repeat a rosary, led by an Indian who knows a few prayers. So they pass the first and second day. One of the relatives goes to town to the office of the civil registry to inscribe the death and to get the death certificate.

151

On the third day the men of the funeral party, taking turns as they tire, carry the coffin on their shoulders to the nearest town. All the relatives and friends of the deceased follow without distinction of sex or age. The procession is led by an Indian playing a rustic violin. Some of the party carry shovels and picks to dig the grave and ropes to lower the coffin. Arriving in town, one of the Indians goes ahead to the church and pays the sacristan two sucres to toll the bells. The cortege waits at one of the corners near the church and does not go a step farther until the bells begin to toll. The funeral procession passes the church to the doleful ringing of the bells. Then it moves on to the cemetery, which is divided into two parts, one for Indians and one for whites. The mourners enter the Indian cemetery and at the foot of a great stone cross rest the coffin, sitting on the ground around it. The women voice a singsong funeral chant, telling of the virtues of the deceased. Some of the group take advantage of the occasion to visit the tombs of their relatives and to have prayers said for their souls. Certain poor people from town are always ready to follow the funeral to the cemetery and to pray the responses in exchange for a little parched corn, bread, fruit, or eggs. Most Indians do not know the Catholic prayers and must hire someone to say them.

One of the Indians raises the lid of the coffin and places next to the corpse a needle and thread. This is so the departed one may mend his clothes when they are torn on the long and difficult journey. The mourner also places in the coffin a small broom of branches, with which the spirit may sweep out his spirit house, and a length of rope which he may use in the next life to carry wood from the mountain to his kitchen. Then all those around the coffin charge the dead with messages for relatives who have already gone on the long journey. The coffin is closed and carried to the grave, which several Indians have meanwhile dug. It is lowered with ropes, slowly, carefully. The grave is then filled. One of the Indians levels and stamps the dirt down with his feet. The earth that remains is formed into a little mound at the head of the grave; this holds a wooden cross, unpainted or possibly stained rose, green, or yellow. On the crosspiece someone, usually the caretaker of the cemetery, writes unevenly in pencil the name of the deceased and the date of the death. On the day of the funeral or the following day everyone gathers again at the house of the friend they have just buried. There a master-prayer, an Indian who knows all the prayers well, directs a last funeral chant to the soul of the dead.

152

In the early morning light the burial party arrives at the Indian section of the cemetery in Otavalo.

Professional mourners are always waiting, eager to offer prayers and eulogies to a departed soul in return for a bit of money, a handful of toasted corn, or a little bread. Their weeping mingles with the melancholy sweetness of a crude violin which celebrates the ascent of a child's soul to paradise.

Holy water is sprinkled on the grave, and the coffin is lowered into the ground.

One Indian shovels the earth back into the grave while his companion tamps it down with his feet.

A brilliant pink cross is planted on the mound. In lead pencil the caretaker of the cemetery has scribbled the name of the deceased and the date of the death.

THE AWAKENING VALLEY

THE CHANGING ECONOMY

THIRTY years ago a white landlord asked an Indian near Otavalo to weave him a length of woolen cloth for a suit. The Indian, who had never woven anything but ponchos and native woolens, set up his loom and with great skill copied a sample of English tweed. The white man was delighted. Now he would not have to send all the way to London for material for his suits. He told his friends. They, too, ordered cloth. The original weaver shared his orders with a friend, and the foundation for a new enterprise was laid.

Before the Otavalos began commercial weaving, they lived entirely by their land, farming only to eat, weaving only to wear and to barter for the bare necessities in the market. Their land was scarcely adequate to support their subsistence economy, and they had no source of cash with which to expand their holdings other than pitifully small earnings from local haciendas or from the disease-ridden plantations of the tropical lowlands.

Now the Indians of Otavalo have an opportunity to make money without working far from home or toiling on the local haciendas. Within a generation a primitive farming culture has been transformed into a manufacturing and trading economy. Money profit for the Otavalos makes it possible to buy more land. In a relatively short time they have developed a new mode of culture that sets them apart from the other Ecuadorian Indians. So industrious, so full of personal enterprise are they becoming, that both travelers and native Ecuadorians are coming to regard them as different from other Indian groups. It is hard to realize that the Otavalos are the same people as the Indians who slave on the haciendas. The success of the Awakening Valley has not yet altered the white man's disparaging concept of the "hopeless Indians." But the characterization no longer fits the Otavalos, for a shift of economy has made them a new people.

One might expect that communities possessing little land, or the least fertile land, would dedicate themselves to industry and commerce. On the contrary, the communities which have the broadest base of fertile land are the most in-

160

The Spanish loom, brought to this continent with the conquest four hundred years ago, is today opening the way to economic freedom for the Indians of Otavalo.

dustrialized or have developed commerce to the greatest extent. This is explained by the fact that land, more than anything else, gives independence, time, and money to the Indian. Only if he has land is it possible for him to acquire the loom, the raw materials, and the intensive training necessary for the production of cloth.

The textile culture of the Otavalos goes back to the earliest history of the Andean Indians. Before the conquest, before the coming of the Incas, the Otavalos and Indians of other tribes in Ecuador were weaving blankets and cloaks from cotton they obtained in trade with the people of the Amazon jungle. The backstrap loom that served them in forgotten times is still in use today in the making of blankets and ponchos. The Indians call these pre-Columbian looms "poncho weavers" to differentiate them from the European loom brought by the Spaniards. When the Indians adopted the llama from the Inca and the sheep and goat from the Spanish, they wove the wool of these animals as well as the traditional cotton.

Soon after the arrival of the Spanish in America the Indians were making use of two looms: the native backstrap and the broad Spanish loom. Today nearly all the Indians of the district of Otavalo know how to weave, but the weavers fall into two distinct groups. Some weave only their necessary clothing, but others weave for sale in the market. The first group uses almost exclusively the native loom; the second group, both native and Spanish looms. The first group weaves only ponchos and flannels; the second group, European-style woolen goods, blankets, shawls, heavy cotton goods, *fachalinas*, and belts as well. The first group spins by hand, a task only for women, using a spindle made of a thin and fragile reed. In the second group, both men and women spin, using a wheel which speeds up the process by at least five times. The first group weaves the wool in its natural colors. The second group is familiar with many kinds of dye.

Not all the Indians in the second group weave the same article or spend the same amount of time on the industry. Various communities have developed specializations. In Carabuela, for example, everyone weaves ponchos; in San Juan cotton goods and *fachalinas* are made; in Peguche, shawls and yard goods for European suits; in Quinchuquí, blankets; in Agato, flannels and yard goods; in La Compañía, ponchos and belts.

The Otavalo Indian is undoubtedly one of the finest weavers of the Andes. The products of his looms are sought in all the markets of the country. Indian weavers have been employed as teachers in the professional schools of Ecuador and in other South American republics as well.

In the Indian home everyone works—men and women, children and old people. For each there is an appropriate task: washing the wool, drying it, picking out the burrs, beating it with a flexible rod to loosen the bits of dirt, carding it to straighten the fibers, spinning, winding the yarn into skeins, dying it, washing it, and drying it again. When the wool has been spun and dyed, the men of the family begin their exclusive work, warping the loom and weaving. Under the porch of the weaver's home all these activities go on at once. The husband may be weaving a section of poncho, a rectangle of flannel for a woman's skirt, or a length of European-style goods, while his wife spins a new pile of wool, and beside her the children pound up dye or card and wind up balls of wool.

The commercialization of the Indian communities is not limited to the weaving of cotton and wool. This enthusiasm for industry has spread to other crafts as well. Communities have taken advantage of available raw materials to develop new industries. The Indians of Punyaro weave baskets of all sizes, forms, and colors, as well as hats and fans, of rushes that grow on the near-by *páramo* of Mojanda. The upland meadows where these rushes grow belongs to an hacienda, so the Indians of Punyaro must work one day on the hacienda to exchange their labor for as many rushes as they can carry home.

The Indians of San Miguel and San Roque weave mats and fans of the broad reeds that grow around the shores of Lake San Pablo. People of other villages make rope from cactus fiber. A few natives of Peguche, the only potters of the district of Otavalo, make use of deposits of clay to produce unglazed baked cooking pots, jars, and plates which are always for sale in the local markets.

Commercial traders have developed out of the rapid growth of home industries. Indians who had previously traded only in livestock and wool now also deal in Indian textiles. These traders buy quantities of ponchos, shawls, scarves, blankets, and European suit goods at the Saturday market for resale throughout the country. Lately they have crossed the borders of Ecuador into Colombia. They carry their wares to far-away Bogotá and beyond to Venezuela and the cities on the Caribbean coast. Thousands of miles from home these Indian traders are a common sight in the cities of the north. They stand in the arcades of busy office buildings or in the squares, displaying bolts of Indian tweeds to the passing crowds. Their white homespun clothes are always spotless under their heavy ponchos, their hair always neatly combed. The many bolts of cloth they carry are always freshly pressed, looking like fine English tweeds.

The Otavalo Indians have convincingly demonstrated their initiative and courage in commercial ventures. Most of the Indian traders both read and write and are becoming familiar with all types of transportation and commercial transactions. In their own country as well as abroad in Colombia and Venezuela, the Indians of Otavalo are admired not only for their picturesque dress but for their cleanliness and dignity and modest behavior.

Twelve pounds of unwashed wool make eight *varas* of cloth, enough for a man's suit.

Wool must be washed in the lake or a stream before spinning.

The washed wool is hung up in the sun or laid out on mats in the dooryard.

When the wool is dry, it must be laboriously cleaned, the burrs pulled out, the matted knots untangled.

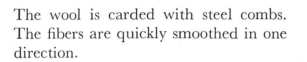

Next the wool is whipped with a flexible rod to loosen every last particle of dirt and to fluff it up for spinning.

The wool is carded with steel combs. The fibers are quickly smoothed in one direction.

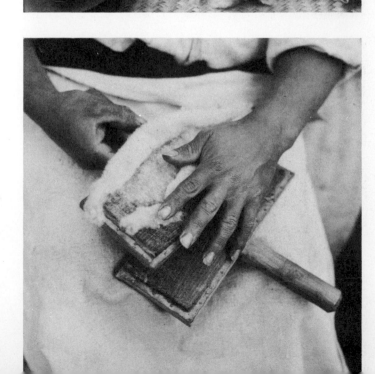

With the palm of the hand the carded wool is made into delicate rolls.

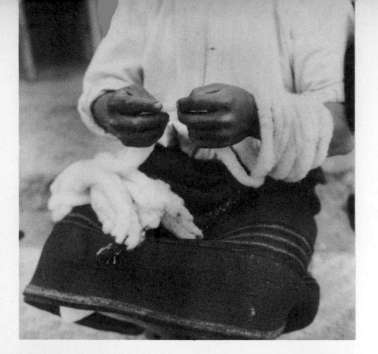

The rolls of carded wool are twisted together in a long loose skein and looped around the arm.

Deftly and swiftly the wool is spun into yarn—heavy or fine, according to the weight of the cloth to be woven.

To spin a pound of wool is a full day's work. Wool from the spindle is then wound into a large skein for dying.

Black-walnut husks are crushed to make a powerful dye, the last of the vegetable dyes still in common use.

Everyone works. There is not a minute to spare. Father grinds walnut pulp. Younger brother cuts up sour oranges to make a mordant for the dye. Older brother weaves down a woolen shawl for a well-to-do *señora* in Otavalo.

The skeins of wool are dumped in a copper kettle of boiling walnut dye, where they boil till the proper shade of olive green or brown is attained.

Before weaving begins, the bobbins must be wound. Yarn from the skeins is wound up on thin reed spools which fit into the shuttle.

A great revolving frame winds up the warp, measuring exactly the eight *varas* ordered by the tailor to make a man's suit.

The finished warp is wound on the loom.

Thread by thread the new warp must be tied to the last few inches of a former warp. Carefully the new warp will be pulled through the heddles and the reeds, and the loom will be ready for weaving again.

Days are spent washing, spinning, and dying wool and setting up the loom. But the weaving itself progresses rapidly. The eight *varas* of cloth may be finished by evening. Then with a thistle comb the weaver raises the nap of the wool and snips off loose threads before delivering his goods to Otavalo.

THE NEW GENERATION

OF EVERY hundred children born in the canton of Otavalo, seventy are Indians. Infant mortality is still high, but once the Indian children have passed through infancy, the well-being of their people assures them a healthy and vigorous future. Their diet is the corn of their ancestors. They eat little white flour, and they get ample vitamins from whole corn and a variety of other native plants. Their health is superior to that of the white and mestizo children of the towns, who live on rice, white bread, and beans.

Children are a happy and functional part of Indian life. From the beginning the child finds a secure place in the family and the community. The infant goes to market on his mother's back. The young child trots along behind when his father and older brothers go to the fields to cultivate or harvest. From his earliest awakening the child finds himself in the midst of a working pattern. He watches the daily tasks, absorbing himself in their reality, and in the many activities of farming, cooking, and textile crafts he finds ample entertainment and material for his imaginative play. As fast as his strength and dexterity develop, he is given real work to do. In all labor the family functions as a unit, and, working alongside his parents, the child learns, one after another, the skills of his culture. Children also participate in the social and religious life of the community, so that they come to adulthood fully versed in the philosophies and traditions of their people.

Indian children not only dress like their parents but also share the same spirit of responsibility in work and have the same aplomb and mature social manners. This maturity comes primarily from their absolute integration into the family group. They are not expected to spend their youth in a child's world of make-believe, for there is only one world in Indian life—the real world of hard work and survival. Into this world children are welcomed for the part they will surely play in the family's economy. They are taught and disciplined carefully with this function in view, and, because they know that their contribution is real,

they learn quickly, take keen pleasure in their tasks, and work with a spirit of genuine responsibility.

The new generation is growing up in an epoch of social change. Every day new techniques and social patterns are thrust into the old Indian world. The children are taking this confusion with a remarkable ease that reflects the emotional balance of their life. With simplicity the Indian parents give their children all the elements of security necessary for a fearless childhood. The new generation faces the complexities of modern culture with confidence and dexterity. The Indian children of Otavalo reflect the enterprising spirit which is carrying their people swiftly into a new economy. With their parents they feel the stimulus of an expanding world. Secure in the strength of their people, they appear to find little conflict in living in a society in full process of transition.

Every year more Indian children go to school in the towns, and, according to the few and incomplete tests of mental ability which have been made, their intelligence is on the average superior to that of white and mestizo children. The national government schools, intended primarily for whites and mestizos, are now crowded with Indian children. Every morning in their well-scrubbed white suits and bright ponchos, they hurry off to school to learn how to make sums, how to speak and read and write in Spanish—and to catch a little glimpse of the vast world beyond their community.

THE CHILDREN OF OTAVALO

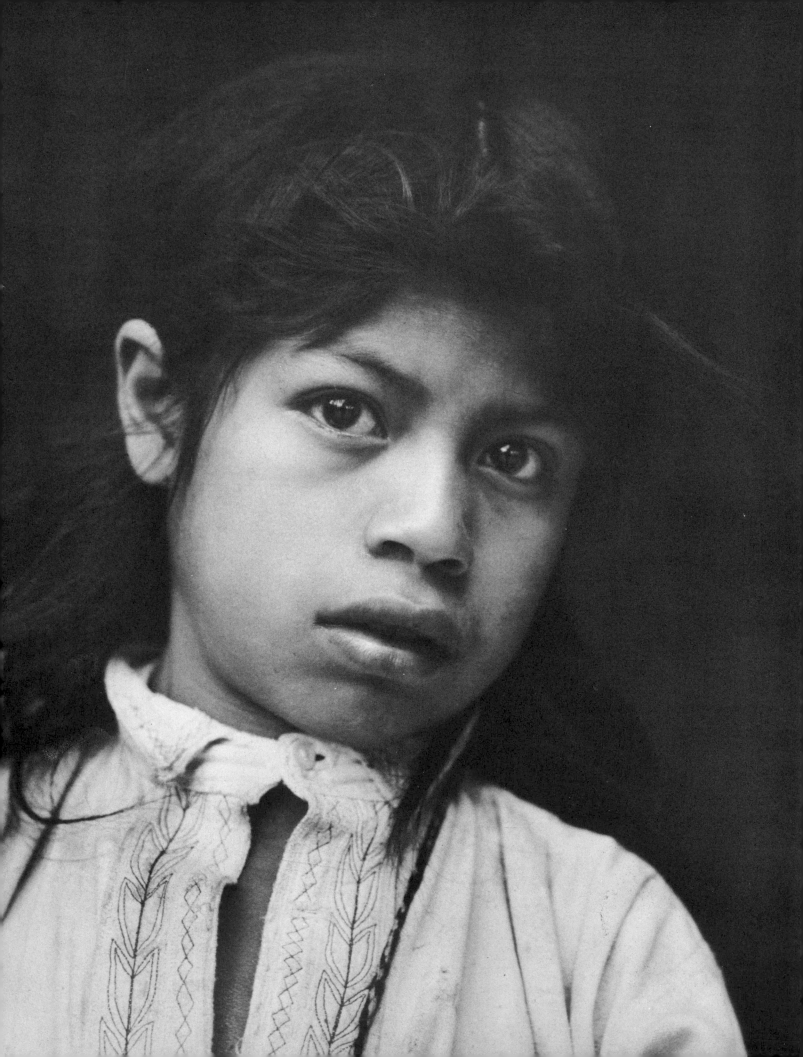

Children's work is not play. It is efficient and productive because it is carried out seriously and with genuine responsibility.

This little boy of three or four has been trusted with the family's pigs.

These two brothers of six and eight have learned to weave straw hats. Now they help their father in his craft, improving the economy of the household.

Village school

HORIZONS

THE success of the Otavalo Indians shows in their wholesome appearance and good health. Both men and women appear strong and intelligent. Their eyes are alert and their bearing upright. By comparison, the white people of the town look worn, discouraged, and apathetic. They seem run down. They are transplanted people. Their culture has degenerated through lack of contact with its Old World origins, but, bred to look down on the Indians, they have stubbornly resisted the techniques or functional cultures of the New World. Thus they have lost the cultural energy they once had as Europeans, but have learned little from the people their forefathers conquered. This, together with poor diet, disease, and the utter lack of economic opportunity, has left them a tired and discouraged people.

In contrast, the Indians have gone through genuinely evolutionary changes. They have gradually absorbed ways of the white world without a disruption of their own Indian culture. They have skilfully adapted modern techniques that fitted into their way of life, eliminating the bad from the good by slow trial and error. No one has forced change upon them or banned their customs and their Indian tongue. As long as the Indians have labored, obeyed the law, and left their sucres at the church, state and church have been indifferent to their fate, so through the apathy of the authorities the Indians have been able to make a unique adjustment—one that is giving them the advantages of the modern age without crushing their spirit. This is certainly a major factor in their survival.

The rapid growth of commercial textile craft has plunged the Otavalo Indians into all the intricacies and pitfalls of business. Sharp enough to see when they were being cheated, they quickly began to protect themselves by learning Spanish and mastering simple arithmetic. In another generation a large group of the younger Indians will be as well educated as the townsmen, for the Otavalos are practical, and, as soon as they see one of their fellows benefiting from education, they too want to read and write. The textile industry itself shows the rapid

194

spread of a practical idea; from one, then two, then three ambitious weavers, it has come to involve whole Indian communities within a single generation.

The white or mestizo townsman is held back by his cynicism. He is sophisticated enough to understand the impossible poverty of Ecuador. He has learned bitterly that honesty and hard work do not always assure success in the extremely limited economy of Ecuador. So he sees no horizon and is often apathetic to opportunity and education. No white man in Ecuador will do work that has customarily been "Indian work." There are many types of labor that even the poorest white man holds beneath his dignity. In the past numerous crafts were considered white men's specialties; no Indian would touch these crafts because of social custom. Today the business-like Otavalo Indians are changing the old ways. Every day more Indians enter into competition with white craftsmen, learning to be carpenters, textile workers, mechanics, charcoal burners, hatmakers, seamstresses, and even traders. But the townspeople steadfastly refuse to do "Indian work." The Indians have no inhibitions against any work. As they develop their own aptitudes, they gradually move in on the white man's economy, just as they gradually move in on the white man's land.

The Indians have what the white men have not—energy and profound faith. The center of their energy and their faith is their land. Not just any land, but *their* land on the slopes of Mount Imbabura. Their confidence in their land is like that of a tree on a mountain ledge. The Indians have their roots as firmly in the soil of the Andes as any mountain tree, and they can take the greatest of humiliations and sufferings as long as they cling to their land. The white men are transient; they are ready to move again. But not the Indians. Come drought or landslide, their roots are in the mountain for survival or extinction.

The white man must look only to his own individuality for strength, and this individualism leads him into greed and antisocial patterns of behavior. The Indian looks beyond himself—out to the lake, up to the glittering peak, and down into the soil—for his strength. He is never alone. His energies are forever tempered by the forces of wind, fire, water, and growth that he shares in common with the earth itself. Despite his success in textiles and his ability to make money, he is still an Indian farmer. All his gain is returned to the circle of his strength—land, crops, and community.

But in contrast to the Awakening Valley of Otavalo, there are the streets of modern Quito, capital of Ecuador. Here Indian men and women in tattered

195

clothing and frayed ponchos carry massive loads like beasts of burden. Their eyes are cast to the ground, their faces resigned and mute.

On an hacienda in the Ecuadorian highlands at shearing time, each Indian is allotted a daily quota of sheep to shear. The *mayordomo* marches up and down urging the Indians on to greater effort, a whip wound around his arm. He is dissatisfied; day will end before the shearing is through. As if lashing a lazy horse, he flays the working Indians, across their backs, across their faces. They never flinch. Animal-like, they work on at the same dogged pace.

Other Indians leave the cold mountain valleys to work for wages on the sugar plantations of the tropical coast country. But before they can save much money, they are ridden with malaria, broken by the heat and the fetid climate. Here many die, alone, far from their beloved mountains.

(These are Indians who have no land. Without land they are without life, without hope. Without land they live as a defeated people. Their spirits sicken, and each year they sink lower into fatal poverty.)

But the spark of Indian energy still burns deep in the hearts of all the Andean Indians. The Otavalos are the most successful, but they are not the only Ecuadorian Indians who have made sacrifices to reacquire their traditional lands. The Indians of the provinces of Azuay and of Loja have displayed the same passionate desire for land and have managed to draw together independent subsistence holdings. In these other groups, however, agriculture has been the mainstay, and agriculture alone has not been enough to break the bonds of poverty. Crafts and industrialization are necessary. The success of Otavalo could be duplicated in any independent community. In time, surely, other Andean Indians will recognize that they can do what the Otavalos have accomplished. The example of the Otavalos will spread to other regions, and there can be a resurgence of Indian vitality throughout the Andes.

What is true in Ecuador is true in all the nations of South America with large Indian populations. Buried under poverty and prejudice, the vitality of these nations is to be found in the Indians. As has been the case with so many other conquerors, the Spanish must eventually be absorbed by the masses they have conquered. The growth of Ecuador must be the growth of the Indians; as long as they are held in subjugation, the cultural and economic progress of the land will be retarded. The destiny of the Andes is in a revival of Indian vitality that will open the doors to individual freedom and national unity.

196

ACKNOWLEDGMENTS

The authors thank The Viking Fund for their interest and support that made the publication of this book possible.

The authors are deeply grateful to the Indians of the Awakening Valley for their invaluable co-operation in the collection of the material. Especially are they indebted to Manuel M. Cáceres and his father, mother, and brothers, of Ilumán; and José Maldonado and his neighbors of La Compañía. They are also grateful to Sr. Aurelio Buitrón, former *comisario nacional* of the canton of Otavalo, and to his hospitable family and to many other townspeople of Otavalo.

Among the friends who have helped in the preparation of the book, they particularly want to thank Dr. Fred Eggan, Dr. Paul Fejos, Wendell Bennett, Donald Collier, Edwin Rosskam, Margué and Joseph O'Kane Foster, Laura and Edward C. Banfield, Bodo Wuth, Ben Shahn, Leo Garel, Madelaine Thatcher, and René d'Harnancourt.

JOHN COLLIER, JR.
ANÍBAL BUITRÓN

198

HOW THIS BOOK WAS MADE

This book is a collaboration in interpretative ethnology, an attempt to combine the method and accuracy of a social scientist with the warmth of an artist-observer. The material was gathered in Otavalo, Ecuador, in the summer of 1946. There were no set limits to the collaboration; each author contributed all he could to each part of the book. Aníbal Buitrón was responsible for the ethnology, planned the general sequence of social and technical data, and directed many details of the field photography. A native son of Otavalo, he furnished profound insight into the complex pattern of white-mestizo-Indian economy and provided invaluable contacts with Indian individuals. The background for the text was gleaned from his keen observations and intense participation in the life of Ecuador. His wife, Barbara Salisbury Buitrón, translated his material into English. Co-author John Collier, Jr., with the help of his wife, Mary Trumbull Collier, did all the photography and assisted in the planning of the book. The rhythm of *The Awakening Valley* was established in Otavalo, and the Colliers carried this pattern through the multitude of alterations and revisions to its present form. Based on the ethnological writings of Mr. Buitrón, the final text of the book was written by Mr. Collier to fit the sequence of the photographs and to interpret the ethnological material as a social narrative.